Break Up
and
Shine

The End Of Your Relationship Is The Making Of You

Marissa Walter

Break Up and Shine

The End Of Your Relationship Is The Making Of You

Copyright © 2017 Marissa Walter
Written by Marissa Walter

Published by Twenty Seventeen Publishing

Cover design by Ventura Creative Projects

ISBN: 978 1 9998138 0 2

Any therapies, materials or techniques suggested or shared by the author are those found to have been of personal benefit. The author does not endorse any particular way of healing, as not all methods will resonate with everyone. Readers are invited to explore available support, and try what feels right for them.

For all of us; the broken-hearted who get back up and start to live life for ourselves again.

CONTENTS

Introduction

When a relationship ends and a partner leaves your life, the sense of loss, abandonment and heartbreak can be devastating. Maybe there were long-term problems in your relationship or perhaps it's sudden and you don't understand why they've gone. You might even have been left for another person, which compounds the pain further still. Whatever the circumstances, and however commonplace broken relationships are, your grief is personal and real.

Seven years ago, I discovered my husband was cheating on me. Working to fix our marriage was not an option for him. It was final and sudden and he was leaving me for her. I was 36 and we had three children; the youngest was a tiny baby. I felt physically wounded; the pain in my chest was like I had been stamped on. The term "broken heart" could not have felt more appropriate. Of course, not all relationships end in such a dramatic way, but however it happens, the end of a marriage, or meaningful relationship, has long been likened to bereavement because it is such a monumental loss; moving on can seem impossible.

In *Break Up and Shine* I aim to show you that by changing the way you think about the break up, you will change the way you feel, and the healing process can be sped up enormously. You will be moving on with your life in ways you never imagined, and you honestly can come to a magical day when you see that it was the *best thing that could have happened to you.*

No one ever tells you how to break up and be happy. We acknowledge that it is going to be a painful process; we might turn to friends for loving support or therapists to help us to come to terms with grief and accept the end of the relationship. However, at the start, few people talk about how it can be a wonderful opportunity to turn your life around, be who you

1

really are and shine your light on the world. This is what I want to do for you.

Break Up and Shine shares with you the emergence of my new self-awareness which followed my deepest despair. I have always been aware of the concept of something 'bigger than me' guiding me; I knew that, as broken as I felt, I had to seize the opportunity to heal and grow from my experience.

It was this belief in my own inner strength, guided by my soul (and a tenacious streak) that drove my rapid healing. I started to write this book less than a year after my husband left me. The speed of moving on is not a reflection of the depth of devastation I felt, by any means. In the beginning, I thought my broken heart could never be mended; I genuinely believed that I could never be happy again, and at times I felt death would be preferable to the pain I was feeling. But something in me knew that I was not on this earth to live my life and seek happiness through another person. I had to grow from this. I had to do more than simply survive the betrayal and heartbreak; I had to work hard to ensure that this episode of my life was a *good* thing. I had to have faith that what was on the other side was better than I could ever have imagined.

And it is! What I have gained, is love of myself, a new awareness of who I am and a life richer, more meaningful and full of happiness than I ever had before. I feel lucky; I am grateful for all I have now and all that is to come. The best part of my life is not over, and neither is yours. *Break Up and Shine* is about helping you realise that.

So, what do you want to know the most?

That it's going to be OK?

That you'll find love again?

That the pain will pass and you'll be happy again?

That there's a reason that this happened?

What if I told you that all of the answers are within you? What if the answer to all the above can be "yes", if you want it to be? Would that be empowering or terrifying?

Most likely terrifying at first, if you're anything like me. Because what we want most when our world caves in, is for someone to make it better. And if it's someone who has left you or hurt you, you want *them* to make it better. But as you work through this book, you will learn to reclaim your power and realise that you have a choice about how you get through this. You will have to look within; something which is not always comfortable, but ultimately liberating. You will find the relief that comes when you no longer feel a victim of what has happened, and instead realise you have what it takes to create the life you want and deserve.

I believe there are three essential components of healing. We need to achieve them all to heal a broken heart and move on with life. These are:

- **Perspective**
- **Self-Love**
- **Forgiveness**

Now, before you shut the book and say, "well that's that, my life is a mess, I'm too broken and I can never forgive what happened to me", stop and ask yourself this most fundamental question:

Would you rather be right or be happy?

I'm hoping that, having picked up this book, you want to be happy. Self-love, is something we *think* we may have, but often we betray ourselves far more than we realise. We tell ourselves we can't do things, we're not attractive enough, strong enough, clever enough, confident enough. We put up unconscious barriers to prevent us from having the life we really want and we allow what happened to prevent us from being happy today. *Break Up and Shine* will show you how these self-sabotaging tactics come up after a painful break-up and will help you to conquer them.

As for forgiveness, it is not as scary or impossible as it seems. It's not even about the other person, but about finding peace within yourself. We will look at it in depth later. Just trust yourself, and believe that once you've started to practise it, your life will be amazing.

Perspective is crucial. It's the small shift in the way you look at a situation which can make it a "good" or a "bad" experience. Stepping back and seeing the bigger picture is in no way negating any of the pain you feel, but it is an immensely powerful tool for showing you that you do have a choice about how you get over your break-up. I will show you several ways that you can shift your perspective.

These three principles form the essence of *Break Up and Shine*. Throughout the book I will share personal experiences and practical advice. There will be exercises after each chapter to allow you to reflect on and clarify what you've read.

- I will lead you through the initial stages of grieving, showing you how you are not alone in your pain, and why you feel the way you do. I will then explain my further stages in the healing process and show you how understanding them is vital to thriving after, rather than simply getting over, a break-up.

- We will look in detail at feelings of blame at the end of a relationship, as well as taking responsibility for unresolved issues from the past, to empower you to live fully for today.

- I will guide you in how to make positive choices when feeling stuck, to resist the temptation to reopen old wounds and to get to a place of peace where your life flows in a positive way.

- I have included a chapter on children after a break-up, because being a mother was such a monumental catalyst for my healing. I also discuss how a self-aware and empowered approach to healing is so beneficial for your children.

- Finally, we will look at how you can find the relationship you deserve, if that's what you want, when the time is right. And the right time is not about a set number of weeks, months or years after your break up; it's when you are far enough along the healing process and are starting to shine!

Using the book

Although *Break Up and Shine* draws on my personal experience you can, of course, apply it to your own individual situation. You may find, for example, that the chapter on children is not relevant to you and may prefer to skip it. Although I refer to my ex-husband, the concepts apply equally for the reversal of spouse gender and same-sex relationships.

At the end of each chapter there are exercises to help you reflect on what you've read. There is space to write your responses in this book, or you might prefer to keep a notebook or diary especially for this work. The questions invite you to think honestly and deeply about your feelings and ask you things which you may not have considered before about your break-up.

You might have picked up this book in the throes of grief and heartbreak and, if so, I send you love and strength to get through those terrible early days.

You may be some time on from the break-up, but feeling stuck and unable to let go or move forward in a positive way. I hope that what I say will resonate with you, and that the tools for healing will help you break through.

You may even be a way into the healing process, and are now wondering what to do with the amazing opportunity you have been handed with your freedom.

Feel your way through this book and find a part that resonates with you. I would suggest reading Part One first, as it lays the foundation for where you are, will help you to see that what you're going through is normal, and is a real starting point for the rest of the work ahead.

In Part Two, any area you pick can be relevant to your stage of your healing, whether deep in sorrow or fighting to fly. You will probably come back to a section again as the need in your life arises. As you work through the book I will remind you periodically to come back to certain exercises, because you will be amazed at how your feelings toward and perception of your break up have shifted since the first time you did them.

Lastly, don't ever be hard on yourself. If you have to put the book down because you just need to grieve and aren't ready to be told you can heal, then do it! But please know that I wrote this book because I was where you are. All I wanted to know at the beginning was that everything was going to be alright, because I honestly could not see how it ever would be. So, if I have one wish for this book it is to let you know that:

You will be OK.

Part One

In the beginning, there is nothing but pain. Real raw pain and an aching in your chest like your heart *is* really broken. It was all I could feel: the sobbing, the wallowing, the screaming anger, the humiliation, the fear and panic; the wretched loneliness.

I, like you may be feeling now, could never envisage a day when I would be glad my husband left me. In the beginning, my world was so shattered I could barely comprehend thought beyond surviving the day. When I did have a moment to contemplate, all my thoughts were fearful, panic-filled monsters – dread for the future looming on the horizon. Grief, anger, financial and practical worries. The story of the betrayal played over and over in my mind. I couldn't see past feeling like this, let alone imagine ever being truly happy again.

Of course, everything was going to be OK. The problem is that, in the beginning, there is no way of knowing *how* it's going to be ok, so all we see is our world caved in. The immediate devastation of the car crash makes it impossible to see a way out. This is normal and you have to allow yourself to feel it, honestly and fully. The period straight after the break-up is the time to grieve, not to deny your feelings and put on a coping face. The stress can make you ill. For me, the immediate physical symptoms following the crisis included a constant knot in the stomach, loss of appetite leading to sudden weight loss, anxiety, panic attacks and a pain in the chest that felt like my heart was sore. You may have felt all or some of these. It is painful and feels unbearable, but it usually eases when the immediate shock subsides. However, it's worth remembering that it's possible to carry longer-term physical symptoms from stresses which have been buried and not dealt with. This is why it is so important to deal with all the emotions and issues as they come up. Your mind doesn't forget your anger, sadness or denial. It just buries them in your subconscious if you decide not to deal with them. And if you don't deal with them, that's when they can manifest into physical tensions in the body. IBS, allergies and migraines are all commonly linked to stress. Keeping your emotions healthy can help keep your body healthy.

What are the emotions you feel?

There are five classic stages of grief as defined by Elizabeth Kübler-Ross in her 1969 book, *In Death and Dying*. The model was later expanded to include other forms of personal loss which included divorce and the end of relationships. The stages are:

- **Denial**
- **Anger**
- **Bargaining**
- **Depression**
- **Acceptance**

Written down, neatly listed on paper it looks like five easy steps from heartbreak to happiness. But of course, it's not like that. You flow in and out of them. You think you've left one stage behind, then something happens to pull you right back there. It can go on for months or even years.

The most important thing to remember, no matter what stage you are in, is to let the feelings be felt. Don't try to suppress them because you think "I shouldn't still be angry/crying/depressed by now". If you are, then you *are* and you must let the feeling be expressed.

However, once you've learned how to, you can help yourself to feel better and to move forward with your life. It doesn't mean that you won't find yourself returning to the earlier stages but each time will be shorter, and they will happen less frequently. There is a way out of the darkness.

So, let's return to the five stages of grief in more detail, to see why we feel what we feel, and how we can help ourselves through them.

Denial: "It's not real; they'll come back any minute"

A strange and possibly perverse feeling I experienced in the beginning, was that I didn't want to hear that I was going to be ok on my own, because I couldn't comprehend that I *was* on my own. All I wanted was for this not to have happened. I was in denial.

Do you find yourself not wanting to hear that the break up could be the best thing that ever happened to you, because a huge part of you still believes that your partner will come back? You might put off making plans and arrangements for the coming weeks or months because "everything will be back to normal by then, when we're back together". Or you may find that when friends talk to you about how you're coping, you aren't speaking honestly because part of you is thinking "we don't need to have this conversation, because s/he'll be back any day now".

This is a wonderful fantasy to cling to momentarily. It's comforting because it allows us to get on with our lives. The hope brings a surge of positivity; we begin to get stronger, improve ourselves. Because in denying the reality of our situation, we are really hoping "if they see how great I am now, they'll want me back". Well, let's look at the possible outcomes:

a) Your partner will come back. If you've worked on yourself from the inside out and are attractive because you are authentic and happy and love yourself, ***and they are worthy of this new you,*** then this could be a gorgeous second time around beautiful relationship. But the chances are, that if you are reading this, then it really is over, which leads us to...

b) You work on yourself; you are happy; you've grown. You don't get back together. You fall apart at the setback, and slip into one of the next stages of the grief cycle. This is normal.

Denial is our mind trying to protect us from that which seems too much to bear. But what our mind doesn't know is that we can cope with the truth. The saying goes "what doesn't kill you makes you stronger" and when you can bear to face the truth that it's over, that the person isn't coming back and yet you are *still here*, still standing with even the smallest conviction to go forward, you can be immensely proud of yourself. The goal isn't to get your partner back; it's to get YOU back.

Anger: "How Could This Happen To Me?"

When trying to heal with an optimistic attitude or self-awareness, there is often confusion surrounding whether you can be "a positive person" and be angry. For me, the paramount consideration is that the anger is present; you can feel it. To suppress it while you contemplate whether you "should" feel angry is to deny part of yourself. Where the spiritually-wise are correct, is that it is bad for us to hold on to negative emotions such as anger, jealousy and revenge. They ultimately serve no purpose but to damage us and our spirit. Holding anger is toxic, releasing it is vital.

So, you feel anger but it needs to be released in a healthy way. There was a time of course, in the early days, when my anger and resentment were directed straight at my husband. It needed doing, things needed saying and it had to come out. But the time for that passes and, in the long run, it is healthier and serves you better not to unleash your negativity onto someone else, however badly they wronged you.

Screaming and thrashing pillows are safe when you are alone. But for me, with small children around, it wasn't practical. Some people find physical exercise the best way to let it out. I found getting a writing pad and scrawling down all my angry words in huge raged writing was an amazing release. I wrote pages of diary in the early months, I didn't hold back or edit or suppress. I didn't set a limit as to how long I was going to keep writing but there naturally came a point several months in when I just didn't need to write the angry words down anymore. I didn't share it with anyone, and eventually, as part of a letting go process much later, I destroyed those diaries, because they no longer served any purpose. But they were a wonderful way to feel and express my hurt and pain without inflicting it on anyone else.

Releasing all the anger in one go isn't possible. It would be too much for a person to cope with! This is why we go around in circles with our emotions. We think we've dealt with it, only for it to come up again and bite us a month down the line. But that's not such a terrible thing. After a month or so we may be better equipped to deal with the newer part of the emotion. It's as if we are being protected by our own minds, which is a comfort. Gradual release is healthy. It lets us get on with life, facing the emotions as they come but not letting them fully consume us.

Anger and rage can feel like they are driving you mad and sometimes you need help to release emotions. Counselling, Emotional Freedom Technique (EFT*) and Sedona Method* are a few which I tried. Go with what feels right for you and what works for you. The goal is to come out the other side of this experience with a sense of peace and acceptance. Not because it makes you a "better person" but because it will make you a happier one.

EFT and Sedona Method are specific learned techniques which help release unwanted emotion attached to negative ways of thinking.

Bargaining: "If I change they'll come back"

One of the things that grief makes us do is to look back with regret. If only I had done this differently, if we had sorted out that issue way back, maybe we wouldn't be here now. One of the hardest things to accept (but which can ultimately bring us the most comfort) is that, whatever happened in the past, we did with the best knowledge, experience and sense of self we had at the time. As a result, things are actually entirely as they should be presently.

Some people try to bargain with their partner; I did. I begged my ex-husband to try to save the marriage. I asked if we could at least try, and that I'd let go if it really couldn't work; he didn't want to. Others bargain with their integrity; they promise to change for the other person. It can never work long term, and your true self suffers when you bargain with it. It's time to notice where in your life you are living for *you*. Not for another person, not for a relationship, but for your own highest good.

If you recognise that you are bargaining and want to stop, that's a great step. If the things that you are feeling, doing and saying are compromising who you truly are then you will know. It requires deep honesty to admit that your relationship wasn't what you thought it was, but it's so rewarding and empowering when you know that you don't have to give anything of yourself up because you are enough without that person.

Depression: "I can't face life alone"

After the initial shock of a split, once the denial and the bargaining fail to comfort us and the anger stops feeling useful, we can go through a period of deep sorrow or depression. There will be days when you feel physically unable to function. Everything looks bleak and there seems to be no positive view to make life seem worthwhile. Sometimes I would feel like I was ok, and then the simplest thing reduced me to an emotional wreck. I remember being out in town one day with my baby, and I walked past a group of young women who looked around the age of the person my husband had left me for; such a small trigger which released memories of my humiliation. I could not function in public that day and ran straight home and cried it out of my system. Feelings of worthlessness and low self-esteem feed depressive symptoms. They make you want to hide away and sometimes, for a while, to curl up and die. For those prone to depression, a devastating loss of a relationship can heighten these symptoms. It's vital to recognise when feelings become all-consuming and to get help.

But it is equally important to recognise that depressive feelings are completely normal. The end of a relationship is a bereavement. You have lost someone you love, you may have lost a home and you may have financial insecurity. Your world as you know it has changed completely in some cases, so allow yourself to feel those feelings. Give yourself permission to cry. Few things are more cathartic than sobbing until you feel drained. The important thing to remember is that these are feelings, emotions. They are not who you are, and you can change how you feel when you decide to. That is the key to getting yourself out of the depressive stage.

Repetition of the stages

As I said before, these stages don't always follow through in a particular order and you may come back to one, more or all of them repeatedly. We get stuck sometimes, and our emotions seem to slip backwards. Things that we think we've dealt with return to hurt us. Thoughts go from being positive and forward looking, to being fearful, depressive and sometimes obsessive. This is perfectly normal because healing is a process, not a one-time event.

But if the way you feel is a *choice* why can our powerful mind not simply create enough positivity and joy to cancel out the pain?

When you live a life that you know and are familiar with, your mind creates a future for that life. Even if you don't have in your conscious mind a five, ten or twenty-year plan, your subconscious has made those plans. In your subconscious mind, you are with your spouse until you die. You imagine any children will grow up together in your family unit; maybe you planned future children together. You have family holidays, perhaps a new house one day, celebrations, careers, highs, lows. You imagined supporting each other through it all.

Then, when that person leaves, unexpectedly, suddenly, painfully, your mind cannot make sense of it. Everything that is in your subconscious mind no longer exists. It has been wiped out and there is nothing to replace it. It is not surprising then, that denial is so very strong in the early stages of grieving. You also start to question your mind. How could you have got it so wrong? If that future you created could so easily be shattered, how can you trust anything you ever believe again?

That subconscious future your mind created cannot just be replaced overnight. It has built up over the years of your relationship. So, never be hard on yourself and feel that you aren't healing quickly enough. The purpose of this book is to let you know there is hope after the heartbreak. But when the bad days come, despite your resolve to be positive, you can now understand why.

Resolving feelings around betrayal

I wanted to write a little about break up due to adultery because it is my own personal experience, and it adds its own specific elements of grief and hurt to the end of a relationship. I became aware that many months down the line of healing and self-love, the affair still tortured me. However much I'd moved on, detached from him, rebuilt my life and found joy in what I had, the thought of the betrayal still had the ability to bring me feelings of revulsion, pain and anger. And to be completely truthful, despite how amazing my life is now, it's still possible to feel a sense of pain to think that someone I once loved and trusted could be capable of that level of betrayal.

In some cases, the discovery of a partner's affair means the immediate end of the marriage for the betrayed person. In other cases, spouses will take back the person who cheated and attempt to heal the marriage. In my case I wanted to do everything I could to save my marriage. But my husband was emphatic that it was over. He tried to lessen his guilty feelings by saying it happened because he "needed to fly", he told me he wasn't leaving for her, but because it was what he needed to do to be "true to himself". He tried to offload guilt by telling me that I was the root of all his issues, and that I needed to take part responsibility for what he did. But ultimately, he left to be with someone else.

It is a devastating thing to face and I have wept with feelings of worthlessness. When you find out your spouse has been cheating, you realise that they weren't in the same relationship as you at all. And who knows for how long? You reopen the wound of discovery again and again, working out the when and how of the deception. It's not useful, but we all do it. It's an obsession. You get into the comparison game, because his behaviour has told you that you are not good enough. That someone else is better. What makes the betrayal so hard to bear is that we buy into what someone else's behaviour says about us. I let my husband tell me that "You are too much of this and not enough of that" and "She is so this, and doesn't do that" and I believed it for a long while.

If, like me, you thought you were happy in your relationship; that despite problems (and which marriage doesn't have those?) it was strong and you had plenty holding it together, you will have been stunned at the sudden ending of everything you knew. And if, added to that, you are told that someone else has taken your place whilst you were still in the relationship, then it becomes easy to start feeling a bit worthless and flawed. Because he left me for her so it must be true, right?

Well, here's another way to look at it. I'm interested in the popular idea that thoughts are energy which can create reality, and the book, *The Astonishing power of Emotions* by Jerry and Esther Hicks, contained a really helpful insight. The theory goes that for a relationship to work, both people must be on a matching wavelength of energy. If one is happy and one isn't, then it's not going to work; sounds obvious, doesn't it? The person who is content in a relationship will be sending out positive vibrational thoughts, to create the future life they want to have. If the other person is unhappy and focused on dissatisfaction, dishonesty and fear (the basis for cheating), there is a huge discord occurring. Though unaware on my part, the split was inevitable. He may have told me that I wasn't good enough for him, but the fact is that he wasn't a match for what I wanted and needed.

Realising this greatly comforted me because it helped me understand that I still get to have the happy life I created with my thoughts, it's just that the person I was with at the time was not a match for that life. If he was, then we would still be together. For me to receive that life, with a person worthy of my love, he had to go. Thinking this way requires a real leap in perspective, but we will come to that in a later chapter.

So where does this leave your battered self-esteem then? Well, what it meant for me was that I no longer believed that he left for someone more amazing than me. The other person is, in fact, irrelevant to who you are. If you learn to keep your energy positive and trusting, despite the betrayal, you will get to have the partner you truly deserve when the time is right. But most importantly, for now, you can love and value yourself unconditionally.

Acceptance...finally?

There will be a point when you reach acceptance that it's over. However, acceptance is not the end; it is simply the end of denial. You can reach acceptance and still feel depressed or angry about your situation. So, don't look to reach acceptance as a point of happiness. You need to go further – that is the difference between simply moving on from a break up and truly shining!

In the next chapter, we will look at my additional stages in the healing process which will gradually help you to leave the earlier heartbreak behind and be truly happy.

✐ Exercises

Spend a few minutes in quiet contemplation to see if you can feel which of the identified stages you are currently in, then write down your responses to the questions on the next pages. Don't reject any feelings which come up, just accept that they are a normal part of the grieving process.

Tip: There is no scoring, analysis or solution-finding required, and no good or bad answer. As you work through the book, you can come back periodically to answer the questions again, and see the progress you have made.

Denial

Does a part of you still want to get back together with your ex-partner, and why?

Are you putting off any important decisions or discussions because deep down you hope your partner may come back?

Anger

Do you feel wronged regarding the end of the relationship, and in which ways?

Are you at all angry with yourself, and why?

Do you feel the need to 'get even'?

In which ways, and towards whom, do you express your angry feelings?

Bargaining

Would you change things about yourself in order to get your partner back?

What would/could you have done differently to avoid the end of the relationship?

What would you be prepared to compromise in order to make the relationship work?

What would you be prepared to give in order to take away the pain you are currently feeling?

Depression

What proportion of the time do you feel low/sad/tearful?

Are you able to laugh at all?

Do you feel able to function in normal daily situations?

How positively are you able to view your potential future?

Take some time to think about what you've written and try to sum up your feelings in this one last question:

What are your biggest fears about being without your partner?

Chapter Two

Beyond Grief

"Turn my sorrow into treasured gold..."

Adele, *Rolling In The Deep*

Within my experience, I began to understand that the stages of grieving (as identified in the previous chapter) didn't end with acceptance, because if I reached acceptance that my marriage was over, but learned nothing from the event, then what was the point? And I believe that there is always a point. When you are in the depths of despair it's not always comforting to hear that "everything happens for a reason". But I think that on a "life is bigger than just me" level, it really does. I believe that all our experiences, good and bad, are there to teach us something; to help us grow as people. The harshest encounters are the tough lessons but they have the most valuable teachings.

I identified my own next stages in the process to rebuilding my life as:

- ~ **Learning**
- ~ **Healing**
- ~ **Growing**
- ~ **Flourishing**

I have always believed in the power of positivity; it's not for everyone but it works for me. It could be argued that if positive thinking works, how was it that my marriage fell apart in such a devastating way? I asked myself the same things; why had this happened, what had I done to deserve such pain? When a relationship ends, especially if drastically and painfully, we never see straight away how it can be a good thing. But I found that once I eventually saw it as an opportunity to learn something about myself, then I began to heal.

It was my faith in the positive energy of the universe that set me on my healing course, and I found that the more I believed that good things could and would happen, the more they began to happen. Of course, it wasn't all happy days from that point on; I had many backward steps, negative thoughts and dark days but as we know, healing is not a one-time event; it's a process.

Believing in something bigger than just what your mind thinks is right for you, is comforting and yet empowering. When you start to believe that life wants you to succeed, you stop feeling victimised and like everything is out to get you. When you put out a predominantly positive energy into the world, what you will receive are predominantly positive experiences. And yes, negative things will still happen but you will start to view those experiences differently by looking for the value in what's happening. There is always something to learn from it.

Learning

Life is constant evolvement, a stream of one event leading to another. Choices made in one situation are not made in isolation; they have effects that ripple throughout your whole life and the lives of those you come into contact with. A major life event like a break-up can be, if you choose to take it, a wonderful opportunity to look at what life is trying to teach you. There are two routes you can go down. One is the negative path:

'I've learnt you can't trust people',

'I'm no good at relationships'

'I've behaved badly and deserve what I got'.

The other path is to see that you are being shown a way to learn something about yourself; life is challenging you:

"Am I capable of getting through this?"

"What am I being shown about taking responsibility for my own life?"

"What brought me to this point and how can I make something good come from such devastation?

Shifting perspective to this far more positive way of viewing the situation allows you to move forward instead of staying stuck. When you are amid the stages of grieving it is very hard to take this path, but the more you practise stepping outside of the grief and looking at the bigger picture, the easier it will become. Perspective is always the key, and I will share with you how I changed my way of viewing situations in Chapter Three.

Healing

Once you start to at least conceive that this ending has happened in order to learn something, then you can take comfort in that idea and begin to heal. But the healing won't happen unless you really want it to. I found that when I started to look at the lessons, there was an enormous amount of inner resistance. You may find that, as with physical healing, it often hurts a great deal before it starts to feel better.

This is when people can give up. The pain of looking inwards, of realising that they must be responsible for making it better, and for making changes, is too much. Often, however miserable it makes us, it's far easier to blame the other person or become bitter and resentful about choices made in the past, than to move forward and let it go. Healing requires courage and strength, and these are qualities that no-one else can give us. They also require self-love, which we will come to in a later chapter.

Growing

Once I entered on the healing path, growth began immediately. By simply allowing yourself to learn and heal from your experience, you start a mind-shift which attracts more positivity into your life. You will begin to act differently because you see things from a new perspective. I stopped seeing myself as the victim of a terrible break up or betrayal, and began talking about my life in a more positive way. Using my divorce to turn my life around for the better became my new purpose. By aiming to become the best version of myself that I could be, I not only made an immense difference to my own well-being and future, but it gave me opportunities to make a bigger difference to other people's lives through choosing to support others going through similar situations.

Flourishing

There will come a point when you can actually admit that the break-up was the best thing that could have happened to you. You may not be anywhere near that yet, but don't dismiss it as a possibility. As wretched as it was at the time, the end of my marriage shaped how my life is now. And what I have now is more wonderful than I could ever have imagined:

I gained a confidence in myself and my abilities that I never possessed before. Five months after my husband left I finally passed my driving test after years of trying and 4 failed attempts. The sense of freedom for myself and my children was, and still is, immeasurable.

I write. My writing started out as a blog to share my experience of healing from break-up with others, and it became this book. I faltered along the way with confidence issues but, again, overcame them because the rewards were more powerful than the fear.

I am a better mother than I have ever been to my children because I'm aware constantly that the break-up shapes their view of the world. It's my job to not let their childhood be a bad experience through no fault of their own.

I have a new relationship. It's more wonderful than I ever could have hoped. It came to me because I challenged myself to let go of the past and never accept less than I deserved.

I retrained in a new career and qualified as a counsellor. I now specialise in working with individuals and couples experiencing relationship problems; as the saying goes, "teach what you know". I could never have become the person I am as a therapist without having been through my own break-up pain.

Moving beyond the initial stages of grief, and into these new areas, are the key to turning your break-up into an opportunity to shine. I can say with certainty that the happiest time of my life is not over; it is now.

✎ Exercises

As in the Chapter One exercise, use this as an opportunity to assess where you are. If you are not yet at a point where you feel you've learned anything or experienced any growth that's ok; you will get there:

Learning

Are you willing to see this as a life lesson, and what might you expect to learn about yourself from this break-up experience?

What are you possibly being shown about taking responsibility for your own happiness?

How are you doing things in your life differently because of what you've learned from the end of this relationship?

Healing

Do you truly believe that you're capable of getting over this relationship?

How might you be holding yourself back from healing? Are you holding on to blame or resentment of your ex? Do you believe, on some level, that being unhappy is all you deserve or can expect out of life?

Growing

At this point, can you see any positive outcomes to the end of your relationship?

Is there any way you could see the end of this relationship from a less painful perspective?

Flourishing

List at least 3 important positive changes in your life since the end of your relationship (*these might be actions or breakthroughs in thought or attitude*):

1.

2.

3.

Now go on to list 5 goals you would like to achieve. They may be huge and seem unreasonable, or they may be the next small steps you feel able to take:

1.

2.

3.

4.

5.

Part Two

Chapter Three

Gaining Perspective

"Happiness is not having what you want, but wanting what you have"

Rabbi H Schachtel

Everything you will read from here requires a shift in perspective, and I will show you four effective ways to do this. Perspective is the key to how your life will be different and happier. True healing requires that you don't try to change things outside of your control, or expect someone else's behaviour to change in order to make you happy; these things never work. But changing how you look at situations, and your inner world, accepting what *is*, and not being a victim of it, is the way you will shine and truly move forward after a relationship breakdown.

This will require you to think and do things differently to how you may have done them before. You will learn that how you respond to something is a choice. It may be your most immediate or natural response, but your response is based on a certain way of looking at something; the way you have previously always looked at it. When you can shift your perspective, you change your reaction to an event, therefore you *feel* differently about it. Life then looks different: better, more hopeful and positive.

1. Be thankful for what you have

One of the biggest perspective shifters is gratitude. It is also surprisingly simple. It doesn't require a huge leap of faith, or deep introspection (which can make you feel uncomfortable). So, we'll start with gratitude as our first healing tool.

You may feel that you have nothing to be thankful for right now. But you do. The beauty of gratitude is that it can make where you are right now feel a very different place in an instant. And as a further bonus, once you start to feel grateful for what you have, you will be in a more positive mindset, which naturally attracts more positive circumstances into your life and therefore have more to be grateful for!

It's the Law of Attraction in action but it is also basic psychology that identifying and feeling good about what you have now can shift you to a more positive-feeling place, and from there it is easier to deal with life and move forward. If you really feel you have nothing to be grateful for, then start with the very basics. Be thankful that your eyes can see, to read this. As simple as that! The list of things will begin to build rapidly. We take so much for granted in our lives, that we forget that life itself is a precious gift and we have the potential to make it amazing. We owe it to ourselves to become aware of what we already have.

A month or so after the split, I began to make a gratitude diary. It replaced the daily diary of emotions I was writing. While my angry diary was invaluable in releasing feelings, it was mostly full of painful emotions. When I started the gratitude diary I felt instant positivity. I would write down anything and everything I could feel to be grateful about, and I found there was a lot: my children, my health, my strength, my amazing friends and my home. Things I took for granted went on the list, like my working laptop and hot running water. It made, and still makes, an amazing difference to my life. I filled several notebooks in a few short months.

Soon I began to find that I was grateful for even the negative experiences in my life, because they were teaching me something. Each level of anger or hurt that I passed through, I became thankful for, because it was another layer released, and another step closer to moving on. Because I was thankful for the good things already in my life, I noticed more good things and saw that they were happening for me all the time. And now when I look back on my diaries, I can see how far I've come since those early days and am grateful for all the learning and growth I've experienced.

Gratitude for me is now a daily practice, sometimes it's conscious, and sometimes just habit. I don't always keep a journal anymore, although I do write a list of things I am thankful for. It mostly just slips into my everyday way of being and feels normal, for example, when I go to the cash machine, it feels natural to say "thank you" when the money comes out!

I often feel a heart-swelling surge of awe and gratitude for where my life is, particularly if I reflect and compare with where it was before. As I moved on from the initial grief, I was hopeful for my future. I had done a lot of the work of healing from my marriage break-up, but there was still a lot of letting go to do. I was yet to be divorced and still wondering how the dream of the life I wanted to create was going to happen.

Life since then has been amazing because I know in my heart that whatever life throws at me, I'll be OK. I will always have something to be grateful for. Gratitude doesn't make challenges go away but you learn to see them as a reminder to get you back on your path in life, by choosing hope over fear; that, in itself, is something to be thankful for.

Beautiful and happy experiences have occurred in my life since my marriage ended. I feel gratitude and contentment for my life at some point every single day. Today, I have a healthy relationship with a man I love very much. My children are thriving. I've become more creative, more confident in my own ability and less worried about what people think of what I do; I earn money doing something I love. I enjoy life more than I ever did before *because* I am grateful.

And this is the vital thing to remember because it's easy to be grateful when your life is flourishing. But the wonderful things in my life didn't just happen by luck whilst I was low and miserable. I had to make the choice to be happy with my circumstances, to appreciate the little and simple things in life; that is what shifts perspective.

Thinking to yourself "what have I got to be thankful for today?" makes you want to experience and enjoy life so that you can answer that question wholeheartedly. It doesn't necessarily mean going out and trying to fill your life with activity to show that you are 'living for today'. It can be as simple as being thankful you have a waterproof coat so you can go walking in the rain. Or being grateful that the kids are asleep so you can curl up on the sofa with some chocolate and a DVD.

2. Choose what you have

Somewhere along the healing process I made a conscious decision to embrace being a single parent. And I mean fully, truly, consciously love my life as a single woman with children. I came to realise that after the end of my marriage, all the pain, the quest to heal, the soul-searching came from one place: resistance to the change in my life; resistance to the present, to what *is*.

Making a conscious decision to *want what you already have* is very similar to gratitude but with more intention behind it. It requires more faith and the ability to see a bigger picture. It can be difficult as it requires some creativity in the mind but it can move you forward enormously in terms of how you feel.

Let's wildly imagine that in the moment my husband left I had simply said, "OK, so this is my life now. I'll just accept and be happy with this". Think of the months of pain and suffering it would have saved, if that were possible! But of course, we carry around history, emotions and fear, reminding us that what happened to us is bad; it will take time to heal. We can't judge ourselves for this, it is simply part of being human. But while this is the normal reaction after a loss, it keeps us in prolonged pain long after an event has passed.

However, if we become aware that we don't *have* to feel terrible about our situation, and we can just accept it as where we are in the present moment, then we have the power to change our lives for the better. This might sound easier said than done but if we make a conscious choice to be happy with what we have right now, and can sustain that awareness *to the best of our ability,* we will begin to feel a shift in perspective which can feel miraculous! It becomes possible to feel peace and joy during what was previously felt as terrible.

In his book *A New Earth*, Eckhart Tolle describes the state in which most people live their lives. We live with the constant unconscious thought running through our minds that:

"There is something that needs to happen in my life before I can be at peace (happy, fulfilled, etc.). And I resent that it hasn't happened yet. Maybe my resentment will finally make it happen".

The 'something' could be a relationship, a job, a better house, a baby, an unfulfilled dream or physical health. Whatever it is, if we wait until we have that thing before we are happy, then something else is guaranteed to come up as the next thing we need to make us happy. Feeling resentful will never bring us happiness.

Knowing that you can choose what you already have, and be OK with that is exhilarating and powerful. It takes a bit of work. You need to be aware of when you are choosing to be unhappy with your life, and the more and more you practise that awareness, the easier it becomes, as you cease being a prisoner to your negative emotions. I do not always find this easy to maintain in my busy life. Being a single parent of three children is sometimes hard beyond belief. But I know deep down that finding peace is in finding perspective, and I am very blessed in so many ways, when I stop and remember. And always, when I am aware of this, my life flows in a more positive way.

3. Embrace Change and Uncertainty

Humans by nature crave security and certainty. One of my biggest life lessons has been learning that I can't control everything and that I must embrace the unknown in order to reach my highest potential. The only things we can ever control are our own thoughts, behaviours and perceptions. I can choose to see the break-up as the most devastating experience of my life, or I can choose to see it as an opportunity to move on to something bigger and better. I read a quote from Deepak Chopra which sums it up beautifully:

"Nature removes the old to make way for the new.
What looks like destruction is the preparation for creation.
Random events are the way station between one form and another.
Your life assembles itself into meaningful patterns.
Perception is a choice: you are free to see any situation as chaotic or creative.
Fear of the unknown isn't innate. It comes from old conditioning and can be overcome."

Being cautious by nature, in the past I have found it so hard to let go and live day by day. I am a planner. I make lists. I like to know that everything is going to be OK. When your world gets ripped from under you and everything is unknown, it is very frightening. On top of the emotional pain, there is the fear of financial insecurity, planning for a future you never anticipated and getting used to new daily routines. I slowly learned to embrace it all. Worrying about something will never make it better; it will only make you *feel* worse. And feeling negative about something is likely to influence a negative outcome.

In his book, *When Everything Changes, Change Everything*, Neale Donald Walsch teaches that it's our perception that change is bad, which makes it so. When we change the way we view change itself, it feels as if a new future of opportunity is unravelling before us. It is an inspirational book which I cannot recommend enough. It is what led me to see that change is not the end, it's actually the beginning, and there is so much more optimism in that viewpoint.

When our path in life dramatically changes, we resist for a while and sometimes for a long while. This is what causes the suffering. The sooner we stop resisting, the sooner we begin to see what's ahead and what's possible. The longer we fight it the longer it takes to get there. We don't allow ourselves to believe that what's ahead could be so much better, and we emotionally exhaust ourselves unnecessarily.

After my husband left, some of the biggest practical changes I was afraid of included:

- Losing weekends with my children
- A change in income because I was a single parent
- Learning to drive in order to gain independence
- Getting a job for the first time since having children
- Organising divorce proceedings

Yet in each case, the *fear* of the change was far, far greater than the reality. Now I can look back on each of those changes, and see ways in which they have made my life better.

These days, I try to plan much less than before, and to act from the heart and from inspiration; I'm learning that life is less stressful and more pleasant this way. I am more flexible with time, whereas before I was compulsive about clock watching! If plans change unexpectedly or things go 'wrong', I remind myself that it might be for a good reason, one which may only become clear later, when something better shows up. I've learned that the future will take care of itself and things fall into place if you make the very best of the present and trust in change.

4. See relationships differently

When we hold on at the end of a relationship and cannot release the other person, we are living their life and not our own. Grief does that to us. Grief is our mind telling us that we cannot be happy without that person in our life. Anger tells us that we are right and they are wrong, and that until they see how wrong they are (and how right we are) then we won't be at peace.

Sometimes the holding on can go on for years after the split. Many people struggle to let go and see the other person leaving their life as a gift. This is understandable; letting go has to be a feeling from the heart, it won't just happen because our minds tell us to. But until you let go, your life will feel stuck.

The pain, the loss and bereavement are real and must be felt and expressed in order to be released. But when the raw grieving has passed, you realise that you need to come back to who you really are. Remember that the source of peace and joy must come from within yourself first. If it doesn't, then anything another person does to 'make you happy' is just an illusion which won't last.

In her book, *Spirit Junkie*, Gabrielle Bernstein teaches that nobody is in your life by accident, be it a friend, lover, work colleague, parent or child. We receive lessons throughout life which help us grow, and return us to a place of love within ourselves. Relationships with other people are a mirror in which we see the parts of ourselves that we can't always see on our own. If the relationship is a positive one, we are seeing the beauty of ourselves reflected back at us. If it is a challenging one, we are facing stuff within ourselves which we need to see and work on. We can never change another person; only they can change themselves.

The important thing to remember, no matter how offensive or painful we feel a person's behaviour to be, is that we have a choice as to how we respond. We can walk away and cut the tie (this is often the best way in a toxic relationship) or we can choose to respond with forgiveness and love. Often, this is thought of as letting someone 'off the hook', but as I discuss in the next chapter, it is not at all. Forgiveness is the way to bring yourself back to a place of peace and happiness so that you can move forward.

When you can step back and see a relationship as an assignment for growth, then it becomes far easier to let go of those which have run their course. We often go into a love relationship believing it will last forever but sometimes, if the lesson has been learned (or it becomes apparent to your soul that you need a new assignment for growth), the relationship will end. Of course, human nature makes us hold on. We want the relationship to continue as we may feel an obligation to a certain person, an outside pressure to keep things as they are or simply have a fear of what life would be like if we let that person go. But all those reasons are causing us to live someone else's life. When we are living the life that our true self was supposed to live, where we can find joy within and fill ourselves up with self-love, then we are free to be without relationships that no longer serve us.

✎ Exercises

Write a list of 10 things you have to be grateful for. Look at it often and *feel* thankful for the things you've put on there.

1.

2.

3.

4.

5.

6.

7.

8.

9.

10.

You may also wish to start a daily gratitude diary to list what you are grateful for each day. You may find the same things come up daily. It doesn't matter, the important thing is that you are practising gratitude and realising that no matter what your circumstances are, they could be a lot worse.

Can you think of any ways in which your relationship was an assignment, and what it required you to learn about yourself?

Are you able to see that the end of your relationship may simply mean that you no longer need that assignment in your life?

What significant changes are occurring, or will occur, in your life because your relationship has ended?

For each of those changes can you think of at least one positive thing which may come from the change?

Chapter Four

Self-Love

"If you're searching for that one person who will change your life, take a look in the mirror"

Unknown Origin

The path to healing involves realising that a lot of the notions we have around marriage and partnerships are illusions. Let me assure, you I haven't become cynical or bitter! I am still a total pushover for romance; I want to be adored, swept off my feet and to share my life with someone who will bring me cake while I watch my favourite chick flicks. But I learned that before this could ever happen, *I* had to be the person who loved me the most.

I used to think that relationships were all about caring for another person's needs and having them do the same for you. I believed that if that wasn't happening then the relationship was a bit lacking in commitment, support or responsibility to each other. In a good strong relationship, of course, each person cares for and supports their partner; but making that the basis of the relationship is a flawed approach. The romantic idea of a couple 'completing' each other, or being what the other needs for happiness, only leads to heartbreak because who can live up to that role their whole life?

It's vital to be happy and fulfilled, **with or without a partner**. This is something we hear so often and you may be thinking: "I *know* this already". And yes, deep down, you do. Few people would openly admit that they don't feel worthwhile as a person without a partner, yet common behaviour states otherwise. As a recently single person, do you avoid doing certain things because you don't want to do them alone? Would you go to the cinema or out to dinner alone? How comfortable would you feel going away for a weekend by yourself, booking a room just for one in a hotel and enjoying a new place?

As part of my mission of self-care, and recognising my own worth, I made myself do those things. It's very hard at first when you've been used to doing things with a partner but the only thing stopping me was a belief that "I can't do these things alone". And when I questioned and changed that belief, new enjoyable experiences opened up for me. Of course, in the beginning it felt strange, but I became increasingly more comfortable just being with myself, and I found I liked my own company a lot.

Since being in my current relationship, I have learned that it is still vital to take time for myself and to do things alone; it's a way of showing myself that I am still my priority. This is not selfish (at least, not with the usual negative connotations that selfishness has). It actually benefits the relationship that you are whole and fulfilled without the expectation or responsibility of the other person to "make you happy".

Reclaiming what you gave away

When you have been left, part of becoming complete again involves looking at areas in which you gave control over to your former partner. Some may be big things, like finances, or decisions over raising children. Some may be smaller; in my case an example was choosing what music I played; I always let my ex-husband decide what we listened to because he didn't approve of my choices. Part of loving myself was to take back the control and to have things the way I wanted and needed.

There is a significant difference between being considerate to someone, and giving away your power or self-esteem to make another person happy or feel better about themselves. I began to see, with my growing sense of self, that I did too much of the latter in my marriage. Of course, it's very common to see these things in hindsight.

My ex-husband believed that it was wrong for me to need anything from him. He made it clear that people should have no expectations of others, and believed that having needs was the same as being "needy". I often felt clingy and like a nag for asking for anything from him so I ended up allowing my expression of needs to be denied. I simply let him carry on pleasing himself while I told myself that I was a good generous wife for allowing him his freedom.

It's true that no other person is responsible for "making us happy" but relationships thrive on a healthy balance of give and take; openness and boundaries; securing our own needs, yet a willingness to acknowledge the other person's. I have since recognised that it is unapologetically OK to need what I need. I also know that I can now give many of these things to myself; I learned very quickly after my marriage ended to give myself the respect, kindness and understanding I needed. I've also realised that, within a healthy relationship, I am allowed to expect things from others; people are free to say yes or no, and I am free to respond to that however I feel.

After a break-up, it's worth thinking about how well your needs were being met, and whether you might have been expecting something your ex wasn't capable of delivering. Always remember though, that your needs are valid despite another's inability to meet them. The pain of a break-up can feel unbearable but if your ex did not acknowledge what was important to you, it does eventually give way to a feeling of relief when you can begin to give *yourself* what you need.

Think about the things you like, the things you LOVE. What do you like to do, wear or eat? Where do you love to go? What do you want to read or watch on TV? What are your ambitions, your dreams, your plans; not the ones that revolved around being a couple but the ones that light you up as a person. You still have them; no-one can take those away from you.

How much time did you ever spend really thinking about these things whilst in your relationship? If you have children, it's easy to let your true self be side-lined, but even without children we can give up on a lot because we are afraid of what our spouses may feel or say about it. During my marriage, my world revolved around being a wife and mother; the break-up became an opportunity to give something back to myself.

Gaining Self-Esteem

I was always a sensitive child and am still a sensitive adult, so intending not to hurt others in relationships comes naturally to me. But sometimes, I have learned, it comes at a cost to me. In the past, I have put other people's needs before my own too many times. This is not uncommon in those with sympathetic traits. We nurture, we cope, we give in and we appease. But when we do that, we hurt ourselves.

There is also the danger of going too far the other way; taking on the confident, projective approach and defending our opinions and rights in a relationship at all costs. Love of the self should not diminish, destroy or hurt another person. True emotional or spiritual growth never involves getting ahead at the expense of others, or your own integrity. We need a balance within us to be well-rounded people with good self-esteem.

In her series of CDs "*Self Esteem: Your Fundamental Power*", Caroline Myss explains that the idea of self-esteem is more than just "sticking up for yourself" or having outward confidence; it is about having fundamental love, and appreciation of, who you are. It is also about being aware and respectful of others' self-esteem, so that you don't compensate for your lack of it by stepping on other people.

I found that once I recognised this deeper concept of self-esteem and my own self-worth, my outward behaviour then changed accordingly; I felt and behaved more confidently. With an increase in self-esteem, you will soon find that you are no longer willing to accept anything intended to make you feel less than who you are.

When my ex-husband left, he went through a stage of being nice to me whenever he wanted something. The rest of the time, his behaviour would range from sullen to obnoxious. Then, if he wanted a favour he would change to being friendly, calm and jovial. If I thought his requests were unreasonable and refused, he would quickly revert to unpleasantness.

After about 8 months of this pattern, I changed and decided I could no longer do this to myself. Part of me had been continually wishing that his pleasantness was a sign that he still cared about me but too often it was followed up with very crass, insensitive behaviour. I also realised that I had been holding out for a genuine apology from him, and some acknowledgment of the pain he caused, but that was never going to come. I had to stop needing that in order to be happy. I had to stop hoping he would change, and instead decide that *I* would change. So, I detached from him.

Now, that sounds easy to say but it is much harder to do when you have a lot of emotion invested in someone. I was stuck and I needed help. By this time, I was increasingly trusting my intuition and was open to new ideas in my quest to heal, so when I came across some information about cutting emotional cords, I decided to try it. Used in some counselling therapy, cord cutting is a technique used to detach you from an unwanted emotional connection to another person. By visualising yourself and the other person physically connected by a cord, then consciously cutting that connection the emotional attachment becomes weakened. Change may not always be obvious straight away, sometimes it takes several attempts. As with all healing processes, it may be that the emotional connection is triggered by new issues some time down the line, and you may have to cut the cords again!

After the exercise, I noticed that I felt very different around my ex-husband. Whereas, before, a large part of my energy was still sucked into his life (on what he had done and what he was doing now), I soon started to feel comfortable detaching from it. My demeanour around him changed: I stopped needing anything emotionally from him or to have him see me a certain way. He picked up on the shift immediately to the point of asking me how long I was 'going to keep this up'. I simply told him that engaging with him was doing nothing positive for me, so I had stopped. From then on, our conversations were about the children and practical matters only. It felt liberating, and it was not long after this, that I felt ready to sell my wedding ring.

Passion and Creativity

It is both exhilarating and comforting to explore your creativity. It is no coincidence that, often, people who have faced major life crises, turn to the arts as a way of expressing their true selves in their healing. As you heal from your trauma and see the bigger picture in life, you might become less self-conscious and care less for other people's judgements on your creativity, so you can express it more easily and are more willing to share it. This doesn't have to mean 'Arts' in the traditional sense. Anything where you feel alive, passionate and connected to life is creative. Your passion could be a sport, a charitable cause or your garden.

So, start by tapping into what you love. Before I found the self-belief to write, my creative loves were painting and photography. I started to change my home and fill it with art work that is beautiful and inspiring. I began to paint and take my own photographs. I started displaying them at home, then found local exhibitions in which to show my work publicly. I started my own website to sell my work. It was irrelevant to me whether the work sold or not, the pleasure and satisfaction was in knowing I had the courage and love of myself to do what I wanted to do. I wouldn't allow a critical person or a critical inner voice to tell me that I couldn't do it.

Finding what your passions are shouldn't be difficult. We often think we don't have any because we repress them in fear of judgement or we convince ourselves that our talents are just hobbies, or "it's nothing really". We don't believe that we could possibly make a living out of them, or use them in any meaningful way.

Creating something for no reason other than to get pleasure from its beauty is very satisfying. Focusing on a project that takes you away from your world, and absorbs you completely, is deeply soothing. The more you do, the more you will want to do; it will be uniquely yours and you will be so proud of it. Don't be self-critical. You don't even have to show anyone if you don't want to. Just do it for the love of yourself.

Having said that, following my creative passions eventually led me to how I make a living. My passion for personal development and growth led me to train as a counsellor, and I continue to write both on my blog and by publishing books which feeds my creative side. Cultivating your self-esteem can uncover a creative soul which serves us all. The things you have learned are things you will go on to share with the world. They can bring positivity to people you don't even know! Don't for a minute think that you can't do anything. The key is to just be yourself.

✏ Exercises

List any examples of when your needs or desires were overruled in your relationship:

Write about times you put your own needs first in your relationship, and how that felt:

Write down any goals you may have wanted to achieve in the past, but never got around to:

What stopped you from doing what you wanted or needed to do?

Do you still need or long for any of those things?

What first steps can you take towards meeting those needs?

Tip: *It can be useful to check in with your list every now and then, to see what's changed for you. As you change and grow, so may your desires. Being able to let go of ideas you've outgrown is liberating and healthy.*

Chapter Five

Making Positive Choices

"May your choices reflect your hopes, not your fears"

Nelson Mandela

If we assume that the life we have today is a result of past actions and experiences, it follows that, in order to have a brighter future, we must start to make more positive choices in the present. However, change can be hard and the thought of becoming someone new might feel daunting.

We all have unfinished business in the past. After a break-up, it can feel like you're going over the same ground emotionally, with the same issues coming up. We carry around feelings which were never expressed; words which were never spoken, things we could have done differently. When it feels difficult to move on, there is sometimes an impulse to reopen an old wound and let all the past hurt be held responsible for how bad life is now. However, dwelling on the past with regret (yet with no power to change it) will leave you stuck. It is useful to look back to recognise how we got to where we are but if we are using the past to deny forgiveness for ourselves and our situation, or to remain stuck in a safe-house because we are afraid of the future, it is precious energy wasted.

To make more positive future choices it's important to learn:

- how and why you might be making decisions based on the past
- how to recognise if the choices you're making are for the right reasons
- how to make a positive choice despite your fears
- how to encourage yourself to keep going once you begin to make changes

Let the past be your teacher, not your prison guard

After my ex-husband left me, I was afraid of being alone. At first, I wanted him back despite the way he had treated me. I believed I could get over his affair because anything was better than being on my own with three small children. When it became clear that he wasn't ever coming back, my thoughts turned to thinking about how I would meet someone new. I didn't begin looking straightaway but my anxiety over being single dominated my thoughts. It wasn't until I started my own personal development, that I realised I needed to look at *why* I had this overwhelming need to be part of a couple. I read books, browsed websites and took online seminars which made me confront my past. I looked back at myself in previous relationships, and identified what I had always needed from them; it was eye-opening. I saw that my own insecurities and feelings of not being enough meant that I needed a partner to focus my energy on instead of myself. I soon came to see that I wasn't ready for someone else in my life just yet, no matter how lonely I thought it would be. The awareness brought me to a choice. I could put my energy into finding a man, and continue the pattern of putting someone else first in my life, or I could spend time enjoying being single for the first time in 17 years. I chose the latter, and I am certain that learning from my past, and choosing to put myself first in this way, led to me being truly ready when I eventually did meet my next love.

The ability to recognise long-standing patterns of thought and behaviour, and altering them to make positive changes, is a gift to yourself. Instead of ignoring my past in order to move on, I faced it and learned from it. I decided to look at the way I had approached relationships previously, and how it had not served me well, but I didn't reproach myself for it; I just realised that it was time to be different. Unless we become aware of our feelings, responses and actions we tend to make choices from past conditioning or old stories we've told ourselves. The more you become aware of *why* you are doing or thinking something, the clearer it will become whether or not you are making a positive choice about your life now.

When moving on from a break-up we often want things which we believe will make us instantly happy. After a broken heart, who doesn't want to reach for what brings immediate relief, whether it's a new relationship, a relocation, revenge, over-indulging or running away and hiding? But it's important to ensure that what we're seeking is truly right for us. If we simply make decisions based on how we've always done things, just to bring instant satisfaction, we will end up with the same results. This is why it is very easy to get into rebound relationships, or make rash changes and life decisions when your world falls apart post break-up. If you haven't addressed the past, then the same patterns will repeat themselves because the unfinished business has not been cleared up. Things won't change unless *we* change.

It takes courage, and it takes trust that sometimes things are happening in the best way even if they don't seem to be. You will sometimes have to face things which are uncomfortable but that's not a reason not to move forward. I had to face up to honest truths about myself and my insecurities. It could have become another opportunity to be self-critical but I learned to just accept my fears and insecurities for what they were and I became more compassionate with myself. When you feel your fears, and choose to move on despite them, then the courage you've shown will make you feel bolder and shine brighter.

Choosing without fear

You might find yourself with many decisions to make after a break-up and you will handle some better than others. Some issues and choices will be practical and require clear thinking (e.g. finances, living arrangements) and some are emotional, needing a more heartfelt response (communication with your ex or family members; what to do with the wedding photo on the bedside table). For quite some time after my husband left, I was unable to even contemplate the idea of divorce. Then, even when I was more emotionally capable, it still seemed too daunting a task to deal with in practice.

I know now that all that was stopping me was fear. Fear of how it would feel to let go, fear of the painful memories and fear of the humiliation of talking about it to officials. I had no idea how it would *actually* feel, I was just afraid of what I was imagining; all I had was one big fat fear of the unknown. Then, one day early in the new year, ten months after he left (and after weeks of procrastination, telling myself I would wait for the "right time"), I just jumped in. I was in town day with no intention of starting divorce proceedings, when I found myself by a solicitor's office and had the sudden thought that *this* was the right time, so that afternoon I called and made an appointment.

The reality of starting proceedings couldn't have been more different to the imagined fear of it. I put down the phone from making the appointment and felt a surge of clarity, lightness and sense of purpose. It felt like a huge blockage had been cleared and the path to my future was in sight once more. By the time my Decree Absolute came through and the marriage was officially over nine months later, I was no longer in a state of grief. It felt powerful and like a release. I felt like I was being set on my way to achieve all the things I could not have achieved whilst I was married.

Moving forward can seem terrifying because it's unfamiliar but let me share with you some things I *never* thought I'd feel OK about after my husband left (yet once I'd done them, they were no big deal):

- removing my ex-husband's name from joint accounts
- clearing his belongings from the house
- giving up my wedding ring
- getting rid of wedding cards and love letters etc
- meeting his girlfriend and seeing their child

Of course, I didn't reach all of these milestones at once; some were within months of the break-up, others a couple of years. The early things were the hardest of all so I see them as my bravest achievements; selling my wedding ring triggered some grief and left me tearful for a few days. But in all cases, I found that the fear of how I would feel was so much worse than the reality. I have discovered that it is the resistance to the change, the fear of what *might* be, that stops us making choices which might be in our best interests.

Whether it's a fresh start, better relationships, a new purpose or a new lover, it will be shown to you and will come into your life when you are ready. This is an interesting concept, as "readiness" is not always on a conscious level. I didn't think I was ready for my marriage to be over but it turns out that I was wrong. Everything that I have learned since then has shown me that my divorce was exactly what I needed in my life in order to become the person I am today.

How do I know if I'm making a positive choice?

There are many things you can do to make yourself feel better after a break-up. Some of them are distractions and some are destructive. What you do to make yourself feel good can sometimes feel like self-love, but can turn out to be self-sabotage. Socialising, meeting new people and throwing yourself back into dating can be wonderful for self-esteem. But going out excessively to avoid facing the sadness only makes it harder to deal with when you eventually have to.

Equally, hiding away to honour your time to grieve may start as an act of self-care but can quickly leave you isolated. What begins as protection from awkward questions and pressure from others, ends up leaving you alone indoors with nothing but your painful thoughts about the break-up.

I found that I needed a change in focus when it came to making decisions in my life. Living from a place of low confidence, worry and putting my own needs last was not working for me. Once I was aware that I was behaving or responding based on old patterns, I could look for a different way of doing things (for example, my choosing not to look for a new relationship until I knew I wanted one for healthy reasons). Pattern changing can be a slow process because it requires noticing our thoughts and behaviour, and constantly being in a place of present awareness is impossible for most people. But when it mattered, knowing I could choose to change was empowering.

Next time you feel torn about a decision or a way of behaving, take some time to quieten your mind and ask the following:

- Is this (decision/behaviour) leading me in the direction of my highest potential or best interests, or am I settling for less than I deserve?
- By doing this, is there any likelihood that it will cause harm to myself or others?

- Where does my responsibility lie?
- Does acting this way fill me with positive feeling?
- Does the alternative make me feel worse or better?
- If I choose *not* to proceed, is it because I know deep down that it's the right choice, or am I simply afraid?

I used these questions as my guide and they helped me to resolve dilemmas around my children's needs, responding to my ex-husband's behaviour and my decision to start training in a new career. Answering honestly will give you a clearer understanding of whether you are following the right path.

How to keep going - Encouraging yourself to make positive choices

Along the recovery road, there might be many emotional and practical setbacks which make you feel as if life is never going to improve. The key to moving forward after your break up is to take small steps with compassion for yourself.

In his book, *The Slight Edge*, Jeff Olson talks about the principle of doing small positive things every day which eventually build into a major change. The theory states that it is the small simple things which, *if we continue to do them*, lead to success. Examples of this could be:

- Keeping a gratitude diary
- Writing a journal of feelings
- Doing some daily exercise
- Eating well
- Taking time out of the day to do something calm
- Remembering to breathe deeply when stressed or upset

However, the downside is that these things are equally easy *not* to do, so we often skip them. If we do commit to stick to something daily, it is also easy to get frustrated when we don't see change happening quickly enough, so we may stop altogether.

The idea is to make the changes part of a daily habit, so that over time it becomes ingrained and becomes part of your normal life. For me, the trick to try to not do too many things at once, otherwise the job becomes too large and insurmountable. When I began to turn my life around, I got caught up in a whirlwind of new ideas about things I could do and be. I set myself daily goals for positive affirmations, keeping gratitude diaries, practising meditation, exercise, writing and painting. These were all wonderful things I wanted to do, with the best intentions, but trying to fit it all in was stressful, and induced guilt when I couldn't do it all with a home to run, a job and three children.

This is where compassion comes in when making positive choices. Sometimes, the kindest and best decision we can make for ourselves is to flop in front of the TV at the end of an emotional or stressful day. We can encourage ourselves to take tiny steps towards our goals (by making them bite-sized and achievable) and be forgiving if we don't manage it. A full hour of yoga or Pilates might be impossible every day but I now commit to stretching every morning before I get up, even if it's only for 5 minutes. I also set a goal of 10 minutes on a mindfulness app every day, yet went for months without even picking it up. However, when I restarted I just accepted that I had slipped, without making myself guilty about it.

I find that the best way to really stick to a new positive choice, is to make sure your heart is really in it and that you are doing it for the right reasons (re-read those "questions to ask yourself" in the earlier section overleaf). When I finally committed to writing *Break Up and Shine*, it was after a three-year gap while I trained as a counsellor. I knew it was the right positive choice for the next step in my life. The intention I set myself to finish it was so strong that daily writing became ingrained as habit; I found that if I wasn't able to write one day, I really missed it.

Post break-up choices may not always be about a big project like writing a book. They might be choices about the way you discuss things with your ex-partner, whether to go and get support for your grief, when it is the right time to think about a new relationship, how to talk to your children about their feelings or taking the next step in choosing to see your life differently.

✒ Exercises

On the following pages, name 3 choices or decisions you need to make about a situation, or perhaps a goal you are considering. Then answer the following questions:

- Is this a decision in my best interests? How positive does it feel?
- What might the negative consequences to this choice be?
- If I don't do this, will I feel worse or better?
- Is fear stopping me from proceeding/not proceeding?
- Am I aware of any old patterns in making/not making this choice?

Tip: Take time to reflect on your answers. Adding a "why?" can be very helpful in order to explore your responses more deeply.

Repeat the exercise for each goal or decision on your list.

Choice/Goal No. 1.

Choice/Goal No.2

Choice/Goal No.3

Think of 3 new **daily** habits you can begin, which will steer you towards making a positive change. These might be related to a specific goal e.g. health or job, or you may want to see a general improvement in your level of positivity, or a shift in attitude. *Remember: keep them achievable but still aim to challenge yourself!*

1.

2.

3.

Chapter Six

Forgiveness

"Holding on to resentment is like drinking poison and expecting the other person to die"

Unknown Origin

I didn't have the choice of cutting my ex-husband out of my life; we had three children and I had to see him regularly. I'm glad in many ways, because it meant I didn't have the option of pretending he didn't exist and living with hidden resentment for the rest of my life. I had to live with facing the person who had brought me the most pain and grief of my life on a daily basis. When I first read the quote above, it touched me deeply and never left me. I realised that despite all the positive thinking, moving on, and self-love I was striving for, I would get nowhere if I could not forgive what happened and forgive what my ex-husband did.

Forgiveness, whether we like it or not (and most of us do not!) is a profound part of healing yet it seems like one of the most difficult obstacles to achieve. I say it *seems* difficult because forgiveness doesn't have to be hard when you approach it in the right way. I hope that what I have learnt will help you see that forgiveness is not as daunting as it initially appears.

It helps to start by looking at why forgiveness is hard; why we don't want to do it. There are several misconceptions around what forgiveness involves. I believed, and I'm sure I'm not alone, that to forgive a person meant that:

- I am letting someone who treated me badly "off the hook"; I'm saying that what they did is OK.
- I must tell them that I forgive them.
- I must admit I was wrong.
- I should tell *them* that *I'm* sorry.
- I am weak or vulnerable.
- I must allow that person back in my life on some level

In truth, if forgiving meant all the above there is no way I could have done it. My sense of justice for myself and my healthy boundaries would not have allowed it. No, forgiving does not mean you need to do any of those things because, amazingly:

Forgiveness is not about the other person at all.

Take a moment to accept the importance of that statement, then let's look at the misconceptions in more detail and see why this is true.

- *By forgiving, I am letting someone who treated me badly "off the hook"; I'm saying that what they did is OK.*

Forgiveness does not mean this. What forgiveness is saying, is that we choose to be OK, *despite* what they have done to us. It's not about the magnitude of the act involved, or, indeed, that person at all. To help me understand this, I reasoned that if people can forgive perpetrators of horrendous crimes (and many do), then forgiveness can't be about saying that what was done is acceptable. My ex-husband cheated on me and left me. The way he behaved was wrong. But I can forgive, because it means I can accept that it happened and still be OK with my life.

- *Forgiving someone means I must tell them that I forgive them.*

Some people want to offer forgiveness to the other person, to say or write the words to them; others do not. There isn't a right or wrong way to go about forgiveness but it's important to stress that just because you haven't told the other person you forgive them, it doesn't mean you haven't forgiven. In some situations, it's emotionally or even physically dangerous to approach your ex-partner after a break-up. Telling them you forgive them can cause more harm to you than good, depending on their reaction. Forgiveness takes place in your heart, whether the other person knows about it or not. Remember, you are doing it for you, not them.

- *Forgiveness means I must admit I was wrong; it means I should tell them that **I'm** sorry.*

No, you don't. The next chapter looks at taking responsibility for your life, and owning the mistakes you may have made in the past. But forgiveness is not about saying "I was wrong" and taking all the blame. When you choose to forgive the situation, you can still be aware of the ways in which you were wronged and feel a sense of justice and protection for that. The two ways of thinking are not incompatible.

- *If I've forgiven someone, then I must allow that person back in my life on some level*

Again, this is a choice and some people will find that following a break-up they can forgive grievances, move on and re-establish a relationship on a different level. But reconnecting emotionally is not obligatory in order for forgiveness to take place. If someone has suffered abuse, betrayal or an acrimonious split, they may choose that the best way to move forward is to cut that tie to their ex-partner. You don't even need a reason not to let the person stay in your life. If it is the best thing to do for *you* then you can still forgive but make a clean break. If you have a tie, such as a child, which keeps that person in your life, it's difficult, but not impossible, with the use of strong emotional boundaries.

- *Forgiving makes me weak or vulnerable.*

Forgiveness does not make you weak. It actually strengthens you. The power gained from being able to let go of a gnawing resentment is immense. Forgiveness allows you to take control of the situation. But contrary to this, yes, it does make us vulnerable (which I don't believe is an undesirable thing, and is not the same as being weak). When we choose to forgive, we open up a part of ourselves which has to see things differently; it requires looking within ourselves and maybe changing who we believed we were. While this can make us vulnerable, it is also soul-enhancing.

So, how do we forgive?

I don't believe that forgiveness is a one-time act. It's an ongoing process; a conscious choice we make in the way we live our lives. One of the things I struggled with was knowing whether I had *really* forgiven, or was just saying I had. Then I realised that it didn't matter; the intention to forgive is more important than anything you can say or do to show you've forgiven; it can even be about ways that you *don't* behave. As I said before, it happens in the heart.

I made a conscious decision to forgive what my ex-husband did very early on; probably when I read the quote about resentment and poison. But the combination of grieving, being triggered by his consistently horrible behaviour and attitude toward me, and a deep sense of feeling resentful about my circumstances made it difficult to believe that I was practicing forgiveness. How could

I have forgiven, when I didn't feel like I'd done any "act of forgiveness"? But I realised that I was looking at it all wrong. I was still believing the misconceptions; thinking I had to *offer* him my forgiveness, deem what he did as OK or have some kind of emotional connection with him again; all of which were impossible for me. I began to look at how I was behaving, and see whether it fitted with forgiveness. I realised that I treated him with fairness, kindness and civility yet I created boundaries to protect myself emotionally. I didn't act in any revenge-seeking ways; I truthfully didn't feel vengeful (although I secretly indulged myself in thoughts that "karma would get him").

Another aspect I found very difficult was forgiving someone who didn't fully accept that they had done anything wrong. I never received a meaningful apology from my ex-husband for his behaviour. He told me a couple of times that he was sorry I got hurt, "but...", followed by justification for his actions. When someone is not remorseful, it's harder to forgive. However, I found that when I shifted my perspective to forgiving the *situation*, rather than the person, it helped me see that it didn't matter that I never received a full apology; it wasn't about him at all. It's also useful to remember that forgiveness is as much about forgiving ourselves as the situation. As we saw in Chapter Three, recognising that all situations in our lives are opportunities for learning, allows us to feel compassion for ourselves.

If the idea of forgiveness still feels impossible to achieve, I've shared below how it came to me one day, deep in thought, after a huge release of grief and sorrow the night before. It's from a very spiritual perspective, which may not resonate with you. However, if a part of it touches you, it's a very powerful way to see a situation from a unique perspective:

Last night I imagined that each person is a soul and our souls are here to teach each other. His soul's job was hard. He had to lower himself with negative energy, cheat himself and his integrity. He had to cause pain and suffering. Souls are loving by nature, and that is a very hard thing for a soul to do. But his soul did this in order that I could grow. His soul gave mine the opportunity to do what it otherwise could not have done. His soul's job was to awaken my soul, allow it to express itself, to learn its true purpose – it may never have been able to do this without such heartbreak. My soul can pay this forward by helping others to heal and find their true potential. So, with an open heart, full of gratitude for the job his soul has done, I let go of my resentment for what happened. My greatest gift to myself is to be able to hold onto this awareness and keep it in my heart because it is the bigger picture that matters, and I feel blessed to be able to see that.

✎ Exercises

Think about the circumstances of your break-up. Is there anyone you feel wronged by?

Is anything stopping you from forgiving that person/those people? If so, what?

Write a little about how it feels to **not** forgive the other person. What benefits are there for you?

What benefits could you see for yourself, by letting go of the resentment?

Can you think of any ways you think or behave already, which show that you are letting go of resentment? *(Remember, your willingness and intention to forgive are as important as your actions.)*

If your thoughts or behaviour are consistently resentful, angry or vengeful, spend a few moments contemplating the quote:

"Holding on to resentment is like drinking poison and expecting the other person to die".

Write a little about how that makes you feel, and how you would like to feel:

Chapter Seven

Responsibility and Boundaries

"Empowerment happens when you face the profound responsibility you have for your own life"

Bryant McGill

You may find this one of the more challenging chapters but please stick with it because what you'll learn is intended to empower you, not diminish your feelings in any way.

Within personal development and spiritual circles, there is a collective understanding that what we experience in life is a reflection of our thoughts and beliefs. In other words, in some way we have created the situations currently in our lives. This can be a hard concept to accept when you find your relationship is over and you are the one suffering, wronged or victimised.

In my situation, my ex-husband was wrong to do what he did; there is no denying that. But making him wrong changes nothing. I could not have believed this in the beginning, but there came a point when I was able to agree, that, from *his* perspective, there were reasons for what he did.

Acknowledging this did not deny or undermine the pain I felt due to his behaviour but being able to recognise it was a huge step forward in my emotional and spiritual progress. It felt like a big "aha" because it allowed me to gradually let go of righteous anger which didn't serve me. I didn't even need to explore his perspective that closely (as his excuses are not my business) but I realised that holding onto *my* story of injustice with such a tight grip did nothing for me.

When you've grieved and ranted, and been right until it hurts, the next step is to work on letting it go. For *you*. It doesn't matter that you know you were right or that other people might believe your ex-partner's version of events. In the end, none of it matters as you can only see it from where you sit, and they will be seeing it from their perspective.

Remember my question at the very beginning of the book:

Would you rather be right or happy?

So, how do you let go and be happy? Keep working on what you've learned so far in this book. Remember that healing and growth are a process, and that the work you've done may need to be repeated as recurring issues come up to the surface. You may have noticed that being asked to take responsibility for your situation can be an enormous trigger for emotions. You might feel anger, injustice or humiliation. Keep working on shifting your perspective, practicing gratitude for where you are and forgiving yourself and the situation.

This is not about victim-blaming; many people have suffered years of unacceptable behaviour before a relationship ends, ranging from slowly-soul-destroying to abusive and dangerous. Acknowledging your part doesn't make what someone else did OK. But, by choosing a new progressive path as a way forward from what happened, you become empowered and in control of your own future. It doesn't change or invalidate what happened but you are no longer defined by the effects of that relationship.

Recognising that the other person has a different perspective is one part of taking responsibility. The next step, and often more challenging, is to look at the part you may have played in creating your circumstances. And, once again, this is not about blaming ourselves. Most of what we create in our lives is done unconsciously, based on old patterns going back as early as our childhoods.

When I look back at my own situation, I am now very aware of what caused my marriage break-up and what my part was. When I found out about the affair and my ex-husband decided he was leaving, he didn't want to look back. I asked him if we could go and see a counsellor to talk about our problems, and he replied; "All of my issues are you". His attempt to put the blame on me left me reeling, and part of me (stuck in my pain and low self-esteem) believed it. Of course, it was just his way to lessen his guilt for having acted the way he did. However, I cannot deny that my old unresolved issues from the past had contributed to difficulties in our marriage, and for that I must take responsibility.

Had we been able to healthily and openly communicate our needs to each other, things may never have turned out the way they did. If I had valued myself more highly, perhaps I would have left him years before he ever got the chance to treat me so poorly. Taking this thinking one step further, had I resolved my childhood issues way back when they first resurfaced, maybe I would have never even met him. If we take the perspective that relationships are assignments, then maybe I called this one in because I needed to learn something in order to grow. In therapeutic terms, I was unconsciously attracted to something within him which allowed me to play out dysfunctional patterns of relationships in my early life. It's not a perspective that everyone would be comfortable with, but I found it empowering; I could now choose how or not to let the past affect me.

This insight didn't happen overnight; it took personal development including months of therapy to see how my personal issues had affected the dynamic of my marriage. I was left with a sense of understanding; not blameful of myself but accepting of why things were as they were.

When we look at taking responsibility, we encounter a lot of "if only" and wisdom of hindsight. But it can't be any other way because, when we are immersed in the relationship, we often don't see what's happening. Looking at your responsibility during post-break-up healing is not only valuable for you to let go of the story of your pain but is immensely useful for moving forwards, so that you don't continue to repeat patterns in future relationships or other areas of your life.

As we start to take responsibility, it becomes equally essential to also discover what had *nothing* to do with us, i.e. once you accept your own stuff, you see objectively and clearly what was the other person's responsibility, and theirs alone.

Giving them back their stuff

Giving your ex-partner back their emotional baggage (in addition to physical possessions) is deeply freeing and sets a clear line between what is yours and what is theirs.

As part of my counselling training, I took part in an exercise where we were invited to return "unwanted gifts", no longer needed, to people. This could be blame or responsibility that a person had wrongly attributed to us, other peoples' opinions or their emotional charges towards us.

In the exercise, you sit with your eyes closed and imagine the person with whom you have an issue (in this case, your ex-partner). Then, bring to mind the "gift" which is emotionally draining you. It might be their anger or guilt. They may be holding you responsible for their feelings or actions, or perhaps they have negative opinions of you which are hurtful. The objective is to visualise yourself holding this unwanted gift in your hands like a physical object, and passing it back to your ex-partner. It might help you to get a strong physical image of what you are holding (I pictured mine as a thorny grey ball which was uncomfortable to hold!). You may wish to speak either in your head or out loud as you do this; you could say something like *"take this back now, it's not mine, it's yours"*, then picture them willingly receiving the gift and walking away. As with the cord-cutting exercise in Chapter Four, you may feel a sense of release straight away, or it may take several rounds of handing back different gifts.

Becoming clear about which issues are yours and which are the other person's is an essential step toward setting boundaries. When we still have an emotional pull or entanglement with an ex-partner, or when we are not clear on our own responsibilities, it's difficult to know where the line of the relationship actually is and to notice when it becomes crossed.

Boundaries

After a break-up, the emotional dynamic between two partners doesn't simply cease to exist. Although your relationship will have become something entirely different to what it was before, there is a period where you still think you know the other person in the same way.

For some time after he left, I realised I expected my ex-husband to respond and converse as if we were still married. As I mentioned previously, when he chose to he would engage in a positive, friendly way which tapped into the natural, comfortable way of communicating we had when we were a couple. But the split, and particularly the manner in which it happened, also meant that he was, in fact, a stranger to me in lots of ways. He had been living a separate life outside of the marriage for a long time and that was his normality now. Because he no longer had to pretend to be my husband, his way of being suddenly became confused and alien to me; one moment he was his old self, the next his lack of respect and understanding of my hurt was bewildering. I had to accept that it was my responsibility to stop emotionally engaging as if we were still something to each other.

This did not happen overnight of course; the grief process, particularly denial, meant it took months for me learn to engage with him as if he wasn't still my husband. But once this way of being began to feel more natural and normal, the difference it made to my perspective was liberating. I no longer had to be concerned with his opinion of me; I could make decisions about my life and my future without worrying about how they would affect him.

For some couples, it is possible to maintain a friendship and certain level of emotional intimacy after a relationship has ended. They are able to negotiate clear boundaries around what they have become; they feel safe to enough explore the reasons why they can't stay together as a couple, and have an awareness and motivation to make it work on a different level.

This was not the case for me. I found the betrayal, as well as my ex-husband's continued disrespect towards me, too much of a hurdle to overcome in order to maintain any kind of friendship. My healing process had seen me grow and change, and he had his own issues (in which I was no longer interested). In all honesty, had we not had children together, it was unlikely I would ever have had any contact with him again, post-divorce. I did not have the desire or emotional energy it would have taken to rebuild a friendship with him. For me, moving on meant clear, civil and respectful communication around the children and nothing else.

My ex-husband wanted our way of relating to be on his terms; he felt I needed to "get over" what had happened and, for the sake of the kids, show them that we were friends. In an ideal world, this would have made perfect sense but I didn't want to make small talk or engage in friendly chitchat with him. I simply didn't trust him, and no longer wanted or needed him involved in my personal world.

It can often be the case that, when you start to change or end an unhealthy dynamic, the other person will resist by holding on tightly and trying to keep things the way that they want them. My ex-husband did this by telling me that my unwillingness to rebuild a friendly relationship with him was hurting the children. It made me realise that the only way forward was to hold strong to my boundaries, and not be manipulated into feeling guilty or like a bad mother.

Now, whenever we meet to pick up and drop off the children, if I need to speak to him, any engagement is respectful but business-like and non-emotional. It's a sad truth that it's not how the children would like it to be but I can't pretend to be something else to their dad; to me, pretending to be friends would be more uncomfortable for them to witness. In Chapter Eight, I talk further about emotional honesty with children.

If you are finding holding boundaries difficult with an ex-partner, it may be worth considering counselling, particularly if there have been control issues in the relationship previously or if you have any underlying low self-esteem or unresolved problems from the past. If an ex-partner is intimidating, manipulative or aggressive, limiting communication to email or factual messages can be a way to keep yourself from being drawn in emotionally.

Other self-help can include revisiting the cord cutting exercise, or practising Emotional Freedom Technique. You could also go back to Chapter Four on self-love and remind yourself of your commitment to live your life for *yourself*, not what another person wants.

✎ Exercises

It is important to be honest in your responses but also to be compassionate with yourself. Acknowledging responsibility should be an opportunity for growth, not a way to feel bad about things you cannot change. Remember to forgive yourself.

Is there anything you could have done differently during your relationship which may have changed how things turned out?

Looking back, can you recognise any signs that your relationship was not working which you ignored? If so, why?

Could you possibly have handled the end of the relationship in a better way?

Since the break-up, have you taken responsibility for any actions or emotions which are not yours?

Reflect on your boundaries with your ex-partner. Are there any ways in which you find it difficult to maintain emotional boundaries? If so, why?

Write a list of things which are your ex-partner's issues, for which you refuse to take responsibility. What will you do in order to give the responsibility back to them?

Chapter Eight

Children

"Children learn more from what you are than what you teach"

W.E.B Du Bois

Getting divorced when you have children is heart-breaking; the sense of personal loss and grief can be compounded by the guilty feeling that you've failed your kids. I recall at the time of the break-up, in addition to my own personal pain, a persistent sorrowful thought running through my mind that *"this isn't how it's supposed to be, this isn't what their childhoods are supposed to look like"*.

So much can be said about children and divorce, that it could become its own book. But in the context of *Break Up and Shine* I want to show that, despite the added implications and complications to a divorce they bring, your children can become a catalyst for your growth.

No parent will ever handle divorce perfectly, and no child will ever come out the other side without at least some small trace of trauma. Part of consciously healing from a break-up when you have children, means finding the right balance between honouring yourself as a person, and being that protective parent who is always working in the best interests of your child.

In sharing my story here, I want to show you that there can be a healthy mix of expressing the emotions of grief, and showing your child that life can still be wonderful after divorce. Moving on in a healthy way can be an inspiration for your children and aid their own healing. It sounds counterintuitive as a parent (as we normally live to put our children first), but after a painful life event like divorce, the more you attend to your own needs the more able you are to be there for your child.

My boys were six and four years old when we sat down and told them that daddy was not going to be living with us anymore; my daughter was little more than newborn. I was so angry that day, as much for them as I was for myself. I grieved the loss of hope and expectations for their childhoods as much as the loss of our marriage.

Keeping it together in the beginning, for the sake of the children, is one of the hardest things I've ever had to do in my life; I was grieving but had to put them first. I was exhausted; all the usual parenting hardships had stayed the same, but I was dealing with them alone and in distress. After being woken relentlessly one night by my baby, I sat and fed her, while inwardly weeping at the injustice of it all.

Without my children I may have succumbed to the despair, bitterness and an inability to move forward; but they were my reason for getting up in the morning. When I wanted to crawl into a hole and not come out, I remembered I had children to clothe and get to school. When I didn't want to eat, my breastfeeding baby forced me to have meals, even if they were tiny portions. I had days where I wanted to scream and smash things, but I had to always keep it in check, because I didn't want to lose control in front of the children.

Trying to control the overwhelming emotions was so uncomfortable and difficult that it left me desperately seeking a more positive and future-thinking way, and this ultimately drove me to turn my life around. I couldn't bear the thought of feeling wretched for years to come. I feared what it would do to my children's lives to see me fall apart or lose control. It became my mission to see that they came out of this as unscarred as possible; I wanted to create divorce damage limitation for them. So, my healing became not just about myself, but my wider role as a mother. When I began my own exploration of gratitude, perspective, forgiveness and self-love, it was not only for myself, but also for my children.

However, I found that this focus on the children's wellbeing wasn't entirely positive; my determination to move us all forward actually stalled certain elements of my moving through grief. Attempting to protect them meant that I didn't let my children see enough of my anger and sadness. I went through the first three years post-divorce never saying *anything* negative to them about the break up or my ex-husband; when their dad behaved unacceptably I justified and excused it to them.

Through therapy I eventually began to recognise what was happening, and I found a way to redress the balance. Not only had my lack of openness with the children stifled my own expression, but it had suppressed theirs too. Children need to see us express real emotion in order to normalise and validate their own. I thought I was shielding them by not breaking down with sadness in front of them but I was actually showing them that it's not ok to be sad about the divorce. As much as I *told* them it's ok to be sad, why would they believe it when mummy hides her tears? And children are no fools; several years later, during a talk with one of my sons, it turns out that he remembered me crying and being sad. It was impossible to hide if from them after all; I simply made it harder for them to ask me about it at the time.

I also struggled with boundaries (which I discussed in the previous chapter) at the beginning of the split. In doing what I believed best for the children, I let my ex-husband have too much time in my home, and too much control over my opinions. Later, in hindsight, and again with the help of a good counsellor,

I realised that I strongly regretted agreeing with my ex-husband in the beginning, not to tell the children why we broke up. I stuck to the story that the split had been mutual and we were both happier apart. It may well have been an easier story for them to hear than one of betrayal and rejection, but as they got older I became aware that when they asked me questions about the divorce, I could never be truly honest with my answers, and about my feelings, because they didn't know what happened; and that felt very uncomfortable.

So, a few years after the divorce, when my eldest child began to ask about why daddy left and why couldn't we still be together as a family, I was able to share with him that I had also been very sad when he went, and that it wasn't my choice. I could say to him, with no vindictiveness, that daddy wasn't happy, that he met somebody else and left because he wanted to be happier. I reassured him that although mummy was in pain at the time, I am happy now. I taught him that it's ok to be sad about losing someone, but that pain doesn't have to last forever; we can learn to be happy again. I can talk to them about the things we have all gained from the break-up. What I've strived to build for my children is an understanding that, just because things aren't the way we originally planned them to be, it doesn't mean that life can't still be wonderful.

Coming from my own childhood family where there were always secrets, and where asking questions was discouraged, I have never wanted this for my own children. Divorce is devastatingly unfair on the kids. Appropriate honesty, given supportively and lovingly with their best interests at heart, is what they deserve. It also meant that I was honouring myself, and not feeling like I was telling a false version of events to protect my ex-husband.

I realise that my children helped me get through the divorce as much as I helped them. To ensure that they were allowed full expression of feelings, I had to allow my own emotions to be felt; we can't teach our children emotional intelligence until we grasp it ourselves. In order to best support my children, I had to accept that my emotional process was a priority. It's important to stress that this doesn't mean that I let them shoulder the burden of adult emotions, for which they were not equipped. There is a balance between offloading grief on your children, and allowing them to see you are a human with emotions.

I began to see that children have their own life paths to lead too, and this divorce was as much part of their life journeys as it was mine. We were individuals within a family unit, going through the same crisis, but each learning our own life lessons. This way of thinking was comforting; although I'm their mother and try to do all I can to protect them, sometimes I simply can't fix life for them, and I must recognise their resilience and ability to overcome hardship. In the same way that divorce did not have to define me, I saw that it didn't have to define my children either. Empathising with them and acknowledging their pain, while teaching them that they could look at this divorce in a different way, was more constructive for all of us than trying to protect them from pain.

Helping my children see the positives in a negative situation has helped to reinforce the teaching in myself. I actively and consciously teach them to see the good in life and look for where they have the power to change things. I recently published a children's gratitude journal, inspired by my children, when I saw what a positive effect it could have on them to notice the good things in their lives. I also teach them about acceptance of the things we can't change, and how that can make us stronger in the end. After the divorce, we carried on some old family routines and traditions, and made new ones as we started over as an altered family; it's important to help children see that change does not always equal bad.

While they didn't choose to have a dad they could only stay with on alternate weekends, they have learned to value the time they spend there. I understand that they miss him between visits and make sure they know that it's ok to express that. They didn't choose to be given another sibling by their dad, while still grieving the loss of him from their own everyday life, but they adapted, accepted and loved the new arrival unconditionally in a way that only children know how.

They didn't choose for their mum to meet and love someone new, effectively ending their deeply held dream that mummy and daddy would one day get back together, but they embrace the relationship with an eagerness and affection for my partner that warms my heart. They understand that they have more family now, more people to love and who give them love. They also have two Christmases every year!

If I look at the post-divorce changes I made in my own life (from learning to drive, to starting a new relationship, to becoming a counsellor and pursuing my writing) I know that I have achieved them for me; it was important to get back the sense of self that I have discussed in the previous chapters, but my decisions have always been driven with responsibility and commitment to my children. I know that I would have emerged from the divorce down a different path, and with different outcomes had it not been for them. Healing and moving on may have been easier without them, or perhaps not. I might have felt freer from the past, without children to tie me to my ex-husband and failed marriage. But a larger part of me believes that my children have given me strength and purpose to move on in a way that I would not have had done without them.

 **Exercises**

How do you think having children has made you approach your break-up differently than you would have done had you been a child-free couple?

How much emotion do you currently allow your children to witness? Is there anything you would like to change about this?

What do you think your children are learning about you as a person?

What do you believe/feel about the idea that the break-up is part of your child's life journey and something which they must experience? How does it feel not to be able to fix the pain for them?

List some ways in which you can prioritise your post break-up healing in a way that will also benefit your children:

Chapter Nine

Finding New Love

"Staying vulnerable is a risk we have to take if we want to experience connection."

Brene Brown

You may feel like the last thing on your mind right now is another relationship. It's a wonderful thing to honour yourself and recognise that being with another partner is not a requisite to healing; in fact, later in the chapter I go on to talk about exactly why being single for a healthy length of time is good for you, and why finding a partner doesn't mean the work on yourself should stop.

You may be struggling with opening yourself up to trust again, particularly after deep hurt. We will explore the issue of how vulnerability, though scary, is the key to loving fully after heartbreak.

However, I start this chapter with a story. I first posted this on my *Break Up and Shine* blog back in 2013, and it still fills me with gratitude and awe to this day to have found someone so right for me after such miserable heartbreak. I'm sharing it because I hope it will inspire others to have faith, listen to their hearts, and let go of the past so that they are in a place where new love has a healthy foundation on which to grow. If you feel ready to think about finding someone new, take comfort in knowing that it really can be safe to trust and love again.

Patience, Work and Cosmic Ordering:
my story of finding love again

Around 11 months after my ex-husband left, I began divorce proceedings. It had been an intense time of grief, letting go and starting to move on with my life. It was January 2011, and with 'new year, fresh start' as motivation, I knew I didn't want to be married to him any longer than I had to.

I began to see that an important part of my future involved having someone to love and love me in return. I wasn't really interested in dating for fun, I wanted to find love. Despite my aversion to the dating game, I knew I had to start somewhere, so I set in my mind an intention that I would go on a date in July of that year.

As the divorce proceedings ambled along, I was faced with further layers of grief to overcome, each part of the process releasing a bit more hurt and bringing up emotional issues to deal with.

Somewhere amid this, a book was brought to my attention entitled, "Calling in The One: 7 weeks to attract the love of your life" by Katherine Woodward Thomas. Despite the title (and the first impression from the front cover), the book was not 7 simple steps to bag a husband! It doesn't teach you skills to be interesting, sexy or funny. In fact, it's a book that takes a lot of courage to work through. It requires determination and a willingness to really look at yourself and your beliefs around relationships. It is kind and encouraging but also asks you to be open and vulnerable.

But it was exactly the kind of necessary work I needed to do to attract the kind of relationship that was going to serve me well and make me happy. As I started work on the book in the spring of 2011, I worked out that 7 weeks to "Call in The One" meant that the man of my dreams would enter my life around mid-June.

I tried to remain open and non-sceptical. I treated the book like a really important project. I did the exercises, pushed myself to get out of my comfort zone when I had to, and really opened myself up to the possibility of finding love, though realistically I had next to zero prospects! I lived in a small town, was a 37-year-old mother of three young children, and I was not in the least interested in online dating. Eligible single men were thin on the ground for me. But I persevered.

July arrived and although I had not given up hope of a date, I was also very much OK with the fact that it might not happen right now (divine timing, and all that). But then on 19th July I sat and simply asked for what I wanted. Out loud. "Universe, please send me a really great boyfriend. Not because I need one, just because I want one!".

That afternoon I was at a friend's house on an entirely unrelated issue, so imagine the shock when she asked me if I knew this friend of hers; apparently, he thought I was beautiful and had asked if he could have my number to ask me out on a date. I was stunned! The perfect timing of it all had me smiling for the rest of the week, and that Saturday night we went on our first date.

In the fairytale ending version, we lived happily ever after. But here's what happened next...

The date was wonderful. I didn't know I was capable of feeling so comfortable and having so much fun with someone new. We both felt the connection, and before we'd even had our second date he had asked me to go away with him for a weekend to a party where I'd meet his close friends. I felt completely comfortable in saying yes.

That summer I fell in love. But there was always a part of me worried that it was too good to be true; wondering what I'd done to deserve being this lucky and meeting someone so special so soon. And when you put those doubtful, fearful thoughts out there, they just hang around waiting for an opportunity to prove you right.

Half way through September we broke up. The circumstances were cruel. Our feelings for each other had not changed, but sometimes forces bigger than you play a part in determining the course of your life. His decision to break up with me crushed me more than I thought was possible, yet the irony was that I respected and loved him more for the choice he had made.

I couldn't make sense of it. I knew in some way I was being tested but I couldn't see how, or why. It just felt so bitterly painful and unfair to have lost someone again, when I thought I was on top of my life. I was torn between letting go and holding on to hope that his circumstances would change. I saw a therapist and sobbed my way through a session. She asked me a question that became pivotal to my happiness:

"How long are you prepared to wait for him?"

*I knew then, that my lesson in all of this was about putting myself first. Not losing myself in love again. Remembering that with or without a relationship **I** matter. At home that evening I wrote down a statement on a piece of paper. It said:*

"If he is the right man for me, please let him come back to me by the end of October".

I had answered my therapist's question. I decided in real time how long I would wait for him, then I would accept things and move on.

The six weeks until the end of October were not filled with endless waiting, expectation or longing. I cried, I mourned. I had an endless supply of love from friends. But I picked myself up; I'd been through worse. I had already learned about heartbreak and was teaching others. I listened to my own advice and continued to work on myself and my happiness.

Towards the end of October, I spent the day with a guy who was a friend. It wasn't a date, but we had always been a bit flirty and enjoyed each other's company. It was a beautiful day and despite the time of year it was sunny and warm. At the end of the day, sitting quietly on the beach, we kissed. I liked him, but neither of us wanted more, we were still just friends. It made me realise how much I missed my love, because deep down I still wanted him back.

Still, I was smiling about the unexpected kissing for the next 24 hours, and that kept me happy and my mind away from heartbreak the next day at work. That evening, the October weather was true to form; it was rainy and chilly. The kids were away and I was cosy indoors. I was alone on a Saturday night, but happy.

When the door knocked my man was the last person I was expecting, despite the fact I'd asked for it. He told me that his difficult circumstances had passed and he was sorry for the way it had ended between us. Ever the respectful man, he had not come over expecting anything from me. We hugged; he was rain-soaked and vulnerable and I felt I had a sense of rightness. I still loved him, but gave him space, aware that emotionally things were not ideal for him. We chatted for a while, then he left.

This happened on the 29th October, and I knew in my heart that he was the right man for me because this was what I'd asked for. As this book is published, we will be celebrating 6 years together!

I couldn't articulate why I wanted to find someone new to love so relatively quickly after such a painful break-up. The usual reasons were there: to have someone to share my life with; emotional and physical intimacy; someone to have fun with; to feel special to someone. But I had a deeper need to be in a relationship, an overwhelming feeling that I just wasn't supposed to be alone. Then I came across the following poem:

You are me, and I am you.
Isn't it obvious that we "inter-are"?
You cultivate the flower in yourself,
so that I will be beautiful.
I transform the garbage in myself,
so that you will not have to suffer.
I support you;
you support me.
I am in this world to offer you peace;
you are in this world to bring me joy – Thich Nhat Hanh

It really was one of the most beautiful things I'd ever read about relationships, and I have it framed by my bedside table. *This* was what I wanted in my life: not a relationship simply to fill a lonely void in my life but a connection with someone that would encourage me to be my best self, and allow me to give that gift of love to someone in return.

Ironically, I found that the test of whether I was ready to be in a relationship was whether I could be happy *without* one. Could the words in the poem be altered slightly to mean the same thing in relationship to myself? Perhaps the poem could read:

"I cultivate the flower in myself so that *I* will be beautiful; I transform the garbage in myself so that *I* will not have to suffer"

"You are in this world to offer *you* peace; you are in this world to bring *you* joy"

I've discovered that the best relationships exist not to make life joyful, but to enhance the happiness that is already there. Responsibility for, and love of yourself is necessary for finding and maintaining a healthy, lasting relationship. Fear of being alone, dependency (emotional or financial) or pressure from other people are not the right foundations for finding a new partner. Of course, you can attract love this way, but the patterns of the past have a way of repeating themselves if lessons are not learned.

Your relationship is just one area of your life. It may be wonderful, enriching and feel vital to you, as mine is to me, but it is not everything and should not define you. Your love relationship is most healthy when it reflects what you are in all other areas of your life. If you feel unsatisfied in your home, job, friendships or family relationships it's tempting to expect your romantic relationship to fill you up and be everything you need. But this is a lot of pressure on another person, to be the happiness in your life. If we expect another to fill us up or "complete" us, then it's only a matter of time before disappointment in the relationship sets in, because we eventually realise that they can't. The goal is not to find the perfect partner and sit back because the work is now done. Once you've found that person, if they are truly right for you, you will inspire each other to want to keep on creating abundance, joy and quality in all other areas of your life.

For me, being ready was about feeling attractive but I don't mean in the feel-good, physical way. I had to look at what I had to offer someone in a relationship as well as what I wanted from one. What did I have that would attract another person? How much of my own stuff had I dealt with, or was I at least willing to work on? How open and trusting was I willing to be? Did I truly love who I was because, if I didn't, how could I expect someone else to love me?

Once I recognised what I had to offer in a relationship, I became ready to work out what I needed to receive from one. I got clear on what was important to me; what I was willing to accept and what I wasn't. I read a lot. I discovered books on manifesting and the Law of Attraction, books on emotional healing and spiritual growth. As mentioned in my story above, the book *Calling In The One* acted as a guide for clearing all the obstacles to allow me to be ready to love again.

It felt like a project but it was work I relished because I was doing something for me. I was creating a happy life on my own terms, following my heart. I was creating a relationship in a way which was new to the past, no longer unconsciously falling for someone who would rescue me from being alone, or give me the love that I didn't get growing up. This time I was looking for someone who wanted me for who I am, and who was worth the love I had to offer.

Being ready for a relationship doesn't mean that you have to be perfectly healed from the past. But it means you need to have gained a level of awareness and acceptance of any issues, change them if you can but detach from them if you can't. Be clear about what you want from a partner but take responsibility for what you need to do for yourself in order to be happy. Don't expect your next partner to make up for all the withheld love and unmet needs from your parents or your ex. That is your responsibility, and the best gift you can give to your new relationship is to be living for the present and future rather than the past.

How do I trust again?

A painful break-up from a committed relationship can create its own particular barriers to loving again. Trust issues, low self-esteem and the inability to break old patterns of behaviour mean that even meeting someone new, let alone sustaining a high-quality relationship with them, feels impossible.

It can be so daunting to put yourself out there to find love again, yet our vulnerability is one of our greatest strengths. We often believe that we risk too much by being vulnerable but when we build a wall around us to protect ourselves from being hurt, we actually risk missing out on so much.

Mistrust causes us to live with the fear that something may be taken from us (physically or emotionally) if we open up. It can make us cynical, suspicious and unable to follow our hearts, as we are afraid it might go wrong, or we'll be let down again.

When I began to open myself up to the idea of meeting someone new, I recognised several fears which may seem familiar to you too:

- Fear of rejection
- Fear of being ridiculed
- Fear of failure
- Fear of being wrong
- Fear of committing and having to follow through
- Fear of being taken advantage of

These fears are so typical that, unless we become self-aware, they can permeate our everyday interactions and jeopardize opportunities to connect with a potential partner. When the barriers are up, our lives become needlessly limited; we don't bother talking to that person because we're certain they won't be interested in a date; we don't show how much we care about a person because we're afraid they won't love us back; we put on a mask when we interact because we think that the person won't like the reality of who we are.

If you've suffered betrayal through adultery or abuse, trust issues become even further magnified. Learning to be vulnerable after deep pain can feel impossible. But it doesn't have to be. If you consciously *choose* to stay open and trusting, you will find that your world changes for the better in ways you may never have imagined. But this only comes from allowing yourself to be vulnerable, despite what has happened in your past.

It's important to use our instincts as our guide, and be aware of why we might be choosing a particular person. Going into a relationship for the wrong reasons may set you up to be let down by someone who doesn't deserve your trust. But equally, you should not let negative past experiences allow you to believe that it's not ever safe to trust again. In order to get to a place where you are comfortable being vulnerable and trusting toward a person or situation, you must first be honest with yourself. It's OK to admit to ourselves that we fear rejection or another failed relationship. Returning to the previous exercises on self-love, perspective and forgiveness will help you to shift some of the self-doubt and help you to make conscious positive choices around opening up to trust.

So, you've let someone in....what now?

Entering a new relationship can be a great test of the "new you". You may have done months or even years of personal development work to get you to a place where you are ready to meet someone new, go on several wonderful dates and get the sense that this person could really be right for you, only to find that, suddenly, masses of your old "stuff" shows up again: Emotions you thought you'd cleared, insecurities and triggers for old patterns of interacting.

Don't despair! Remember the idea that relationships are assignments? I believe that in a new relationship we sometimes face things so that we can see what we've learned from the first (or second or third) time around. We are tested to see whether we might respond differently, and what this means. My current partner likes to tease for fun. Because of my past (childhood and previous relationships), being teased can be deeply uncomfortable, and triggers all kinds of issues around not being respected or listened to. So, when my partner was having his fun one day, and took it too far, I got really upset; it reminded me of previous unkindness and criticism masked as "having a laugh". The old me, would have internalised the hurt feelings, and accepted that I was being too sensitive and "couldn't take a joke".

However, I could not do this to myself anymore. I needed to know that I could speak up if I didn't like something, I also needed to know what was going on here. Was it the same as the teasing I'd experienced before; unkind mocking disguised as fun? Well, I soon found out! Having burst into tears and asked my partner to stop, I discovered how absolutely mortified he was that he had upset me. He was genuinely playing, and didn't know that it had gone too far. He was really sorry, and I was slightly bemused by the fact that I had become so upset. This was the test. I needed to see that this behaviour in my new relationship wasn't the same as in my old ones, and I could only do this by confronting it. Old patterns may be triggered over and over in new relationships, but it is up to us, with our newly-found awareness, to work out what is really going on. This is why it's so important to keep working on ourselves even when we find new love. It's a way of ensuring that our self-esteem and integrity are enhanced, not replaced, by a new partner.

Even when a new relationship is going well it can still give rise to insecurities if we don't keep up the important work of checking in with ourselves; what we want out of life and who we want to be. In the blissful honeymoon stage of my new relationship, and even beyond, I frequently experienced an unease of "this is all too good to be true". My range of fears included: not being healed enough to cope with a relationship; feeling I wasn't right for him; feeling I might lose my sense of self in a relationship; fear of being hurt again, fear of letting him down, feeling I didn't deserve to be this lucky.

"Too good to be true" is a common phenomenon that almost everyone experiences when life is going exceptionally well. It's underpinned by a belief that life should be difficult and, somehow, we don't deserve to be happy without a catch. In his 2009 book *The Big Leap*, Gay Hendricks describes the "Upper Limit Problem", where we reach a certain amount of happiness or success in our lives, then self-sabotage because deep down we are afraid of achieving what we really want. My Upper Limit Problem started to kick in as soon as I realised that this relationship might turn into something long-lasting and wonderful.

It was only through continuing to do this self-development work that I managed to push through these fears. Gratitude and perspective, forgiveness and self-love were just as vital being in a relationship, as they were when I was healing from a broken heart. I used my questions from the 'Making Positive Choices' chapter to help me realise what I wanted from life and to consider whether being in this relationship could give that to me. I had to be prepared to be honest with myself and accept that, if things weren't right, I couldn't stay in it to avoid being alone again. Thankfully, I discovered that all was well; just more fears and potential for sabotage had come up to test me. My new relationship wasn't "too good to be true" after all, it was just good. And I finally realised I deserve that.

✎ Exercises

If you have started dating (or are considering it), what are your reasons? How did you know you were ready?

Can you name anything you have learned since your break-up which will make a difference to how you view a new relationship?

Can you name any specific fears you have around meeting somebody new?

How does the thought of opening yourself up emotionally to someone new feel to you?

Can you list some ways in which you can keep your sense of self-love, identity and ability to meet your own needs while looking for, or beginning a new partnership?

Your Time to Shine....

Having read and worked through *Break Up and Shine,* my wish is that you now realise that the world hasn't stopped because your relationship has ended. You have the power to do more than simply move on from your break-up. You can make it the start of a wonderful opportunity, whatever that means personally to you and your life.

I had no special magic which took away my grief and made me get over my divorce (as much as I had wished it at the time). I'm just an ordinary person who decided that I wasn't destined for misery just because somebody didn't want to be with me. Once I'd made that decision, my life began to change. Use your reflections and any new awareness from the exercises to keep moving forwards and discovering what you want from your life now. Remember to repeat them as often as necessary.

We all have so much to experience from, and contribute to, the world. You have the strength to get through your sadness, anger and disappointment. You have the ability to live the best and happiest part of your life from now on, and I wish you all the joy you deserve moving forward. It all starts with a choice and I know that if I could do it, then so can you.

Acknowledgments and Gratitude

Thank you to everyone who has ever read, shared, commented on or contacted me through the blog; knowing that what I write is useful and supportive has given me the encouragement to complete *Break Up and Shine*. Thank you to my wonderful friends and to Simon who all believed in my ability to write this book; always supportive and never doubting it would eventually be published, despite the delays. Thank you to everyone involved with me throughout my counselling training; tutors, colleagues, clients and my fantastic counsellor. Delaying writing my while I trained, meant I learned so much about myself and what I could offer, and this ultimately made *Break Up and Shine* a better book. Thank you to Nicky New for her editing and feedback, interspersed with encouraging comments and smiley faces! Thank you to Anna Ventura for her commitment to get the look I wanted for my book cover. Thank you to my children who have always inspired me to be my best self, and are patient and ever-loving even when I'm not. And a final acknowledgment of thanks to my ex-husband, because one of the most painful chapters of my life became my chance to grow and shine.

Marissa Walter is a counsellor specialising in relationship issues, and is the writer of the inspiring blog Break Up and Shine.

www.breakupandshine.com

She has published articles on *tinybuddha.com* and guest written a contribution for the 2015 book "*365 Tiny Love Challenges*" by Lori Deschene.

Also by Marissa Walter:

Five a Day Thank You Journal: Helping Kids Increase Positivity through Gratitude

www.fiveadaythankyou.com